IT'S IMPORTANT I REMEMBER

CORTNEY LAMAR CHARLESTON

It's Important I Remember

poems

CURBSTONE BOOKS / NORTHWESTERN UNIVERSITY PRESS
EVANSTON, ILLINOIS

Curbstone Books
Northwestern University Press
www.nupress.northwestern.edu

Printed in the United States of America

10 9 8 7 6 5 4 3 2 1

ISBN 978-0-8101-4964-9 (cloth)
ISBN 978-0-8101-4965-6 (ebook)

Cataloging-in-Publication Data are available from the Library of Congress.

for the ancestors and the elders

for my history teachers in- and outside of classrooms

for my nation within my country

for my firstborn, who all of this is new to

CONTENTS

~~05.25.2020~~

the opposite of love

~~09.17.1787~~

insure domestic tranquility

~~11.08.2016~~

inevitability

~~11.07.2020~~

the thing with feathers

~~01.06.2021~~

to be determined

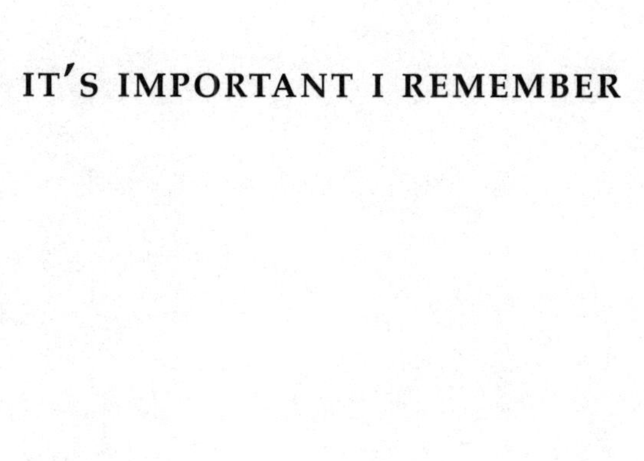

IT'S IMPORTANT I REMEMBER

It's Important I Remember—

tack time back to event. Here, immigrants take citizenship tests but natural-born babies get byes. The act of remembrance is meant to signal profound love for this country in the first instance that's betrayed by the second. The line separating the scenarios has the function of a hyphen. *Black* has my favor for this reason—it invites wholeness. Where the body politic meets body, I swell purple. The aches in my joints don't foreshadow coming rain but

coming sorrow. Jesus wept when Michael Brown was mowed down, but that will not be on the exam. Our new president of sadness is a natural fit for high office because he makes sadness, just more politely. Nobody really had to convince me to vote for him, and many people want me to love him faithfully, but I don't adore who I'm not present to finally bury. My favor doesn't come free of expectation, not anymore. Guilt-ridden people line

up for my forgiveness, mistaking me for a murdered man. There's a line for each of us, a script to recite; America writes dialogue for every role but heartland villainy, which improvises. That's also not on the test. I favor the right answer, not the correct one, if that makes sense. We are natural lie detectors, my people. The instinct sprints in our veins like the color of love or a first-choice Kool-Aid. There are hundreds of bodies inside this body,

thus the vestiges of chattel slavery are visible; most simply fail to see a body for the ship it is. *They* is singular and plural with purpose. I am a dotted line between realms drawn by an invisible hand attached to no god. For the love of money we were cuffed and herded here under hull; we were free labor but not *free*, confined to being colleagues of mules and cattle. Duly, I've a natural affinity for the avian. The eagle *is* on the exam. Symbols often hold favor

over substance. Some wanted our first black president to be our last. Favor never came to us from him, yet men shouted *race-monger* in the legislative body.

Surprise in the past shaping the present spills privilege. Hate is a natural resource that we won't burn through in a near-enough future. I pull line after line from the Constitution, making all the holes in it more evident. But for our grace does this place remain a place at all, though we never fell in love

with letting things slide the way it may seem to some.   To use *nigga* in love
honors survivorship, not victimhood. Bless the real ones to whom I ask a favor:
    Shutter the prisons, but not before the killer cops go in for long bids; but
not before we make homes for those homecoming at last.   The human body
is like a warm cabin and mine is heated by a wood stove, a humility. A line
of inquiry leads me to an old black woman in a rocking chair with a natural

tang to her talk I love: In seeking answers within, I seek her.   In my body,
but few elsewheres, there's solidarity until ammo opens me.   On the line
is who power will favor.   The test is oppositional, as no citizen is natural.

~~03.11.2020~~

this country is sick

It's Important I Remember

THAT I CAN NEVER WASH MY HANDS ENOUGH—

our most touching overtures toward each other
have turned against us, targeted us
for shortness of breath and breadth of lifespan.

When I tell you it's dead outside, I mean people
are dying outside—getting zipped up in plastic bags
and set aside for collection like household waste
that fills land's cavities rotten.

The sun is almost enough to sucker me into
believing that it's a lovely day, but
Bill Withers himself just withered away.

There is no music in a moment like this:
the governor restricting our movements while
conducting the state's response to the pathogen.

We shutter inside like secrets a house keeps.
Our sense of connection cuts in and out.

I work from home with spotty Wi-Fi
since capitalism will get very ill from the virus
but, given its youthful vitality, will probably not die.

Instead, it will probably be the Postmates man
pedaling down my windswept block.

It will be the poor and the black and the brown,
the delicate old ladies and their husbands
who beat the Nazis before their grandsons
became sympathizers in their twilight.

We're in the *Twilight Zone* with zealots.

The panic sets in and people pack the gun
stores to pick up higher firepower and ammo.

The proper term for this isn't *pandemonium*—
it's *predictable*, the highest spike in sales
since the black guy got elected to term number two.

I smell blood in the water even if I can't see it.

I'm running the water so much, rinsing
my palms red with soap and scalding spit
from the swan-necked faucet.

There's no grace in surviving
so comfortably as this.

There's no god that wouldn't have considered
sending the plague up to our doors and,
in some cases, beneath them, as if to say
we are what Egypt was in the scriptures.

The back of our dollar argues affirmatively:
that one thing we hold dear that the greatest number
of hands have touched, either contaminating them
or being contaminated by them, if there's a difference.

A man can make money and money
can make a man—make a man sick in the head
and make a man safe from a sickness
all at the same time. Yes,
I'm absolutely ashamed to admit it:

When I thought about sacrifice the other day,
I thought of myself first and foremost.

It's Important I Remember

THAT THERE ARE SEVERAL WAYS TO KILL HOUSEPLANTS—

watering too much.   Watering too little.
Not providing enough sunlight or providing too much.
        Letting cold air overcome them.

With concern pitched at the right octave,
the green, gangly things will survive, if not thrive,
alongside us and, thus far, ours are holding on for dear life.

                              I can tell by the way she pencils in their height
against the wall over time that there is an act of substitution at play,
the kind of thing that makes me dream of what's to come
even if I know there will be so many more complicating factors,
                                        so much less room for error.

In the streets outside our shoebox, the people shout, unknowingly
paraphrasing a Greek poet: *They tried to bury us,*
                                          they didn't know we were seeds.

As they pass by, headed toward city hall,   masked
by cloth and by night, a flower bud   is startled
open on our windowsill to her   genuine delight,
but I'm elsewhere fiddling   with the thermostat,
panicked over a single   degree of difference

                                as if—

It's Important I Remember

THAT SURVIVAL IS A MATTER OF LUCK—

it just so happens the bad thing didn't happen to me.

Odds are odd that way.

That lightning would twice touch the same spot is rarer than rare,
like the lottery drawing the birthday you played for forty years.

Keep in mind that the likelihood of witnessing rain today is nonzero.

What the chances are and whose they are.

The problem with probabilities is people.
There was mercy only because there was a threat so close by.

Solving for *x* is easier than solving for *why*.

When the laws of mathematics meet the laws of the State.

What's *in the cards* is stacked in the deck alongside what isn't.

Think of all the possibilities,
but don't think of them evenly.

Hope is fundamentally a calculation of difference.

If you don't have certainty,
what you have is faith.

So many of us have gambled on God and won.
So many have lost.

It's Important I Remember

THAT *DARKNESS* AND *BLACKNESS* AREN'T PERFECT SYNONYMS—

but the Venn diagram is a perfect circle.

I poke my neck through the hole of comparison like a hula hoop,
hoping, under no circumstances, that it ever cuts as close

as the collar of the dress shirt hanging in my closet
feeding moths a feast in lean times.

It is the dead center of summer.
We are centering the dead.
The dead are everywhere,
surround me.

There is the virus and the viral video
and they are not the same,

yet the Venn diagram is a perfect circle.

A question is what a ventilator would've done for Mr. Floyd.
An answer is what it means to have mercy to be able to give.

A question is why the Lord put his knee on my cousin's neck.
An answer is what happens when mercy is not received.

A stethoscope and a handcuff
both have a radius;
they are circles that overlap perfectly
around darkness.

Eight minutes and forty-six seconds
is not enough time

to say hundreds of thousands of names
scratched out in less than a year.

The great hoax is the thing that kills us:
The pathogen is just an accomplice;
the officer is just an accomplice.

Blackness encircles
my circle.

Systemic, *systematic*, *symptom*: The syllables slush in my mouth,
spike my sugar skyward.

They say the sitting president is not the disease but of the disease;
they say the disease is not of the president but is the president's:

The Venn diagram is a perfect circle.

My body overlaps hers in bed, both in common need
of touch to turn away from ethereal existence.

Our aims and anxieties are always
in between us, a commonality like our bed.

There isn't a crisis I know of that isn't existential
and therefore something beyond what *exhausting* can describe.

The person that feels everything
and the person that feels nothing:

The Venn diagram is a perfect circle.

What they look like isn't what they are,
but they are indeed what they look like.

It's Important I Remember

THAT WHITE BLOOD CELLS FIGHT DISEASE WITHIN THE BODY—

there are multiple types fit to multiple functions.

Basophils inflame
allergic response. Neutrophils neuter
bacteria. Eosinophils smite
parasites and cancers. Lymphocytes execute
carriers of familiar antigens. Monocytes evacuate the dead
cells, call for backup.

These are the body's answer to invisible threats.

At this point in the pandemic of the century,

we've lost well beyond our conservative projections,
approaching millions deceased exponentially.

Where personal boundaries are drawn determines
who has our sympathies and who doesn't
within the body politic.

The mask has been ripped off because it's ineffective
at convincing there's any empathy this far into the regime.

Sickness spreads not by droplets in the air,
not through bodily fluids or the contact of skin on skin—

but the beatings, the bullets, the bomb threats clarify
it's the lack of recognition within the body itself

that illness is present that allows it to persist, to thrive,
for the simple fact that the fighting agents see themselves

as white when they are, technically, colorless
unless a dye intervenes

under the scrutiny of a microscope and practiced eye.

It's Important I Remember

THAT BEING ALONE AND BEING LONELY AREN'T THE SAME THING—

a distinction I know well from unwellness.
And, also, that the only thing lowlier than me
in measure of loneliness is an empty chair—

I linger on the image when President Biden,
again, alludes to the multitudes missing
from their kitchen tables in his public address.

The illness that took them I'd taken in already,
months ago; it didn't take me out, thankfully, though
there are faces I'll never forget matched to names
having no reason, now, to be said. I stand up and walk

away from the screen, turning back briefly to find an
impression of me calcified on the couch cushion, dented
from hundreds and hundreds of days heavied by mass death.

Without ever looking in an honest mirror, I could tell you
my lethargy isn't aesthetically pleasing. My gorgeous
wife researches online as to where we can purchase
replacement foam to fill in the damage idleness has done,
and I reflect on how much I appreciate a smooth surface,
like her nourished flesh resting against my own.

The times I've been a wrinkle in a plan are hard to admit
and easy to count, but that's something I refuse to do
since my mind is too formidable with tabulation:

        the weeks it's been since I've seen you;
the months it's been since we've spoken;
        the years it's been since anything
other than the end of something dear.

I glance at the woman beside me who hasn't wavered,
who stays where I can reach out and confirm her,
but when I tried the other day, in the widening gap
between night and morning, my hand
fell through hers without a flinch of notice—

and I felt not unlike an apparition, but more like
the atmosphere in this era of empirical misery:
weighty, yet unable to precipitate a form of water.

It's Important I Remember

THAT THINGS ARE GETTING BACK TO NORMAL AROUND HERE—

the trains are busy with bodies. There's an ass
in every seat, hands on every inch of railing,

and small acts of consideration are now
optional, says the poster by the sliding doors.

I keep my face covered among the commuters,
which means my feelings are well concealed as well.

Displeasure, *disdain*, *defeat*: All of these are
possibilities that will not pronounce themselves to
any anonymous companions, even through my posture.

My headphones rest over my ears, as is habit,
and sing the songs I need to hear
whenever I need to hear them;
on this particular ride, I press pause

just as I'm sold to release my job, as the
people-watching grows intensely interesting.

The proper definition of panhandling
requires the act take place on the street, so

underground it's just plain begging, and he is
on his knees in the middle of the train car,

a maneuver I've not seen before in this situation,
a bit of flair I admire for not having it myself.

But, ultimately, it doesn't matter. It rarely does.
New Yorkers aren't always friendly, but they are kind

enough not to make eye contact and pretend
a connection that isn't there and never will be.

Not being from here originally, I am kind
in a Midwestern manner: I maintain
an emptiness in my weathered wallet

so that I do not have to ignore,
so that I do not have to lie.

~~01.20.2017~~

under new management

It's Important I Remember

THAT THERE WAS NO POET AT DONALD TRUMP'S INAUGURATION—

the first abandonment of an action taken by his professorial predecessor, though its importance bypassed the press because, as it stands, only three prior presidents invited a poet to summon whatever better angels exist in America.

The relationship between the poet and the State is tenuous; taxes are paid one way in bills and paid back the other direction in pennies. There isn't true love between the two, just a dependency of one on the other. And yet I should've mulled over what it meant that it was no loss to the incoming regime that poetry be rendered invisible on that national stage.

Carnage, if I recollect correctly, was the theme that day—an end to American carnage. But, of course, the calamities only continued under the new president. Hell, they accelerated.

I watched the car mow that woman down like a leaf of grass, she and some thirty others, all for having that rare combination of conscience and courage, resisting the white supremacists stomping through Charlottesville.

I penned a poem about what I witnessed, how I witnessed, through what eyes and social position.

You can still read it on the internet. The link is not dead, nor you, nor I, not yet.

"The magic power of a poem consists in it always being filled with *duende*, in its baptizing all who gaze at it with dark water, since with *duende* it is easier to love, to understand, and be certain of being loved, and being understood, and this struggle for expression and the communication of that expression in poetry sometimes acquires a fatal character."

—*Federico García Lorca*

Everything was copacetic in the beginning: just me and one word at a time, messing around on sheets of scrap paper, arguing and making up again. Writing was, as with all new romances, a source of great excitement. It was 2009. Young Jeezy's president was black and his Lambo was blue. I'd voted for the black dude, the blue candidate, the past fall: It was my first time voting for anything of consequence, a college first-year holding on to the audacity of hope, certain the jobs would return by the time I graduated with a degree that designated me an attractive hire.

In the worst-case scenario, I could stay on my parents' health care plans until age twenty-six, so I was *gucci*; I was good. I could maybe take a semester abroad and not have to be ashamed of admitting I was American after our misguided Middle East invasions (thanks, Obama!). But then white folks started dumping tea in the harbor again. Then the troops never came home like they were supposed to. Then that rent-a-cop killed that boy and didn't go to prison. Then the movie theater got lit up like the marquee outside one dark night. Then the elementary school got lit up in broad daylight, and then the real cop caught a big boy's body somewhere near St. Louis, and then we took to the streets. Then another school, another cop, another march in another name. Then this ass clown showed up right on cue—caked in makeup, coming down that escalator as cameras flashed—to launch his presidential campaign with a tirade tilting at windmills, leaning into tyranny. And through all that unrest, my boo thang and I had only gotten more and more serious, by which I mean we became more like the world in one another's eyes; we became more and more each other's world, burning in desire but burning nonetheless.

From Merriam-Webster:

A *metaphor* is a figure of speech in which a word or phrase literally denoting one kind of object or idea is used in place of another to suggest a likeness or analogy between them.

A *simile* is a figure of speech comparing two unlike things that is often introduced by *like* or *as*.

America is a house on fire is an example of metaphor.

America is like a house on fire is an example of simile.

The difference between metaphor and simile is often one of urgency.

The difference between metaphor and simile is one of conviction.

Poets are masters of metaphor, if they are any good.

The body of murdered Spanish poet Federico García Lorca has never been found: It's the loot the fascists' dogs never returned to retrieve.

Francisco Franco, *El Caudillo*, forbid speaking of the assassination throughout the life of his repressive regime; all that power and he could still feel shame in some measure, I suppose.

The leftist, however, left behind his many writings: a body of work. His ghost has been translated into several languages, English understandably included; it only makes sense that his body can be translated from one context into another also—from one country into another, across a border that is only an idea of separation, not the genuine article.

The new administration's attempted travel ban targeting majority-Muslim countries rightfully received the early headlines, but I also remember them trying to pull the plug on the National Endowment for the Arts around the time Trump revised his original executive order, a perverse nod to the importance of craft. I recall, like, three people I talked to were upset about arts funding being stricken from the budget and they may have all been me. Perhaps not enough of us citizens realized what becomes possible when you turn off the little light bulbs over people's heads—except for those struggling artists, those tortured poets, who couldn't pay the utility bill anyway.

The pundits are saying we're entering uncharted territory now: constitutional crisis; moral crisis; manufactured crisis after crisis after crisis.

I know why the caged child sings: for their mother, their father.

An invisible hand softly strums a Spanish guitar.

We hand out Grammys and Oscars and wear pins that say *Time's Up* two years after the *Access Hollywood* tapes—his own words—failed to take him down. And we do mean it when we say it, but sadly less than we mean to protect normal business operations. And we understand the phrase on its face, but something else is really being said: Nobody ever gives a damn until it's too late.

It's been proven time and again that true evil has a long lifespan; I hope that carnival barker goes before I do just like I'd hoped to be good enough to die young at one point, when I still tilted toward possibility as a voter. But to be safe, in case my virtues precede me, I'll leave these little bones of English behind for you to find, praying that they help you find your way through—in and then out, like a bullet that hits one person and then another behind them.

"The *duende* . . . won't appear if he can't see the possibility of death, if he doesn't know he can haunt death's house, if he's not certain to shake those branches we all carry, that do not bring, can never bring, consolation."

—*Federico García Lorca*

It's Important I Remember

THAT A TANK HAS NEVER STOPPED THE LYRIC—

as the same book they slammed shut on Lorca
I spread open like anatomies of ascension,

and from those pages the fascists' bullets fly
into my marveled mouth like zealous insects.

I gag. I cough, not unlike an exhausted trigger. I spit
into my hand, then glance down to find the barren shells

of sunflower seeds, and then I laugh.   I laugh
like a dangerous man who knows that he's dangerous

to somebody who's dangerous to everybody.
With this, I am changed inside, as other things are changed—

as blood is to vapor; as a full magazine is to an empty one.
But in leaving the bones of letters behind, I become idea:

something that no soldier or assassin can assign death.
A body is a body;   a body of work is so much more.

It's Important I Remember

THAT PEOPLE WHO SEARCH FOR ME ON GOOGLE ALSO SEARCH FOR TERRANCE HAYES—

who I searched for on bookstore shelves in a leap of faith
off one poem that sucker punched my softest, blackest spot.

When people search for me,
they search for Evie Shockley,
who I searched for after workshop because the way in which
she pulled language out of a dense feeling seemed cousin
to mine, a feeling in the stomach so dense that light can't escape it.

When people search for me,
they search for francine j. harris,
who I searched for online after reading the poem about Katherine
with the lazy eye, or francine herself, or whoever I knew from
my own life that could fit the outline traced around another's absence.

When people search for me,
they search for Patricia Smith,
who I searched for in the crowd after her panel because she's
been a teacher to many I'd want to teach me and comes
from the city I love, where teachers like my father strike
to strike back against attempts at their diminishment.

When people search for me,
they search for Danez Smith,
who I searched for at the fish fry some years back, because
I once found a friend who'd found a friend in them.

When people search for me,
they search for Jericho Brown,
who I searched for after a happenstance dinner one night deep
in Brooklyn because it was dark everywhere, and I needed
that laugh more than I needed food or a stiff drink to bring
my walls down while my government built one.

When people search for me,
                                        they search for Ross Gay,
who I searched for after that backyard reading in Portland
for no other reason than he seemed to have the rare kind
of eyes that see people as persons all their own.

                                                When
        they search for me,
        they search for them;
        they search for themselves,

on their own behalf. And
                                                when
        they search for us,
        they search for poets

of a certain ink. And
                                                when
        they search for poetry,
        they search for answers.

                                                When
        they search for me,
        they search for them.
                                                When
        they search for us,
        they search,

ultimately, for questions.

They search poets.
                                        They search me.
They search a certain ink.

They search me.

They search people

who know to question, even if they know nothing else,
because suspicion is where a scheme

starts to fall apart.

It's Important I Remember

THAT EVEN DONALD TRUMP DIDN'T BELIEVE HE'D WIN THE ELECTION—

this was first reported in the weeks following his upset victory, in *Politico* or somewhere of reputable standing, though the headline was quickly buried by the gravity of the moment. Still, this report suggests we should consider two things to be true: that none of this was inevitable and that the forty-fifth president of the United States is as ignorant as his critics claim he is, though not in the way they typically mean it. Far from stable genius, even while purposefully stoking flames with hot mics, he underestimated what white people could do when heated to a boil, whereas some of us have the burn marks to prove it.

Allow me to make a joke here: If hindsight is twenty-twenty, then only four years are required for a robust democracy to die. This is the part where you laugh or this is the part where you do something. Sorry if you missed your chance to strike, but another is rounding the corner now, and now, and now again. Do you feel that, comrade? Do you feel the urgency with which a heart beats life out to the border of nerve?

There's a rhythm to surviving catastrophe that you need to tap out with your toes, trust me—this is what my people do to make sure our feet are still on the ground after all these years. But don't worry over us: We're going to do what we've always done and that's weed across this beautiful land, maybe light up a new leaf with our unconditional beloveds. This isn't to condone breaking the law as it's written but I also don't condone the law as it stands—in deliberate antithesis to what I am, not what I do—so I'll leave you to weigh my chances just how I do when considering any kind of movement in the presence of a cop, one pulled toward me like the moon to our fevered planet. I believe this is apt comparison as I am my mother's whole world, my father's, my family's.

Let me guess: You're sincerely sorry I must shoulder this anxiety, but it's not what I need to hear right now. I need to hear you were in the forest when the tree fell and made a sound, a plea. I need you to realize the tree is actually a man I could've been and could still become, a poet put down like an empty pen when I'd been led to believe we're needed now more than ever, but I doubt it—

unless we're writing in blood.

~~06.01.2020~~

made in America

It's Important I Remember

THAT DROPPING A BOMB ON AN OCCUPIED ROW HOUSE IS UNCONSCIONABLE—

but it happened, here, on American soil:
West Philadelphia, 1985,

the year most of the country remembers
for the Chicago Bears' "Super Bowl Shuffle,"

reducing the massacre to a footnote
of a footnote of the Reagan years,

the nation gingerly marching rightward
wearing a smile made for television.

The sky was blue that day, as blue as a cop
or a Democrat's tie on the debate stage.

Wilson Goode was Philadelphia's mayor then,
Democrat, black if you can believe it, and I can

because racism is no stranger to blackface
whether by face paint or by borrow.

A bomb in a satchel bag: I can believe it
because I'm black, actually—it fell from the sky

like a Berlin care package back in '48,
the sky that was as blue as a cop,

after Philly PD had already put tens
of thousands of bullets through the walls.

The bomb broke the row house; flames broke out.
The flames broke into the neighboring homes

like the thieves they were until another sixty-odd
houses were stolen in one move. MOVE

was the target, the alleged terrorists though also
the ones without a bomb to let fly.

Everybody in the row house was MOVE.
Everybody in the row house was Africa.

Everybody black is Africa.
Everybody black was in that row house,

that row house in the birthplace
of the United States of America.

Eleven of thirteen died, five of them children.
One woman went to prison

for not frying in the fire. She was not a cop,
not anyone receiving pay from the city;

she was Africa, so
she was everybody black.

America   bombed my house in a former life.
America   imprisoned me in a former life.
America   killed me—a kid—in a former life.

In 2008, when I touched down in Philly for school,
Obama was running for president, a Chicago Democrat,

black if you can believe it.
I could see the smoke from the window

as the plane descended to tarmac.
I was reminded who I was,

that I once lived in the birthplace of America
until I was moved out, to put it mildly.

Been on the move ever since.

From body to body:
every body that's black.

It's Important I Remember

THAT WHITE MEN KILLED MARTIN LUTHER KING JR.—

that when the doctors opened his body by blade like an envelope
they found the muscle of his relentless love to resemble that of
a man much older than thirty-nine years, and though there's
no forensic doubt that the soliloquy of a single bullet fired by
a single shooter from a boarding room window took Martin
off the world stage, only a wide-ranging conspiracy concocted
in the halls of government, and in police stations, and in places
of industry and commerce—from big-city factories down to small-
town mom-and-pop shops—could have explained the heart of a black
man short of middle age hopscotching over entire decades of vitality into
a casket towed by two humble mules through the streets of his hometown.

In the event it wasn't fully evident yet, racism is the sweeping conspiracy
of which I speak, though in most instances, in these days that I dwell in,
following the martyrdom of many and made possible by spilled blood—
like a Christian's salvation is believed to be—it's also the unspeakable,
the unallowable public articulation. It's what the most scathing words of
his prophetic speeches and sermons were aimed at, the ones they clip into
sound bites that distort his key message, which is, also, key to a massive
cage, thus helping prevent our escape from this vicious reality how they
deftly slip away from hard facts. By *we*, I mean trafficked Africans, and
by *they*, I mean *the* Americans—

the opposite side of the hyphen
balancing these lenses on my broad nose, what gifts me a cold blue
iris to compliment the brown one on the other side of my face. This
is why only one eye ever waters, secretes a solitary and righteous
stream down my cheek for the body of the latest felled with only
their bare hands as a weapon in the name of self-defense, and those,
even, completely unused. None of this is unusual in this nation, to say
the least: Let the record show our dear republic has a history of killing
peaceful protesters. And let the record show that I, too, have been to
the mountaintop, but I went only to holler toward the horizon, waiting
to see if the heavens trembled or if I'd bear the brunt of silence and
learn, for certain, the one I've prayed to doesn't see me in His image,
that when I get to the promised land, it will not be measured in acres
but in feet: just enough to fit me lying flat, stiff as the wood of a cross.

It's Important I Remember

THAT NELSON MANDELA WASN'T NONVIOLENT—

because there's a tendency to misremember things
about this man— as we do with every other—
a man that America once titled a terrorist.

It's a paranormal phenomenon from what I've read—
the *Mandela effect*—but that doesn't refute the pictures in our heads
being authentic to their time like grain is to film.

Factually speaking, he did emerge from prison that day in 1990,
triumphant and brass like a trumpet, his hand in Winnie's
hand, held high above their heads
as if a fight had been called favorably in the late rounds.

Twenty-seven years of imprisonment
washed most of the race from his hair; hard labor
in the limestone quarry pulled his eyelids as close as the lips sit
in the absence of expression, but, even still,
light had a slim chance through to the soul.

And chances were slim

the day his cell doors slid back: The bullets were still
flying over Bishop Tutu's protestations,
the world's eyes watching for godlessness.

By that point in time, Madiba was about as dangerous
as my grandfather was after he'd already been my grandfather
for two decades, more war stories than war
making found inside his mellowed musculature.

The old revolutionary's release from confinement was an appeal
to finally put the guns down against apartheid,
an attempt to pinch quiet the bomb's fuse.

To my mind,   when people recall overhearing he passed away
while behind bars,   this is what they may be stumbling over:

I did not plan it in a spirit of recklessness,
nor because I have any love

for violence. I planned it as a result
of a calm and sober assessment

of the political situation that had arisen
after many years of tyranny,

exploitation, and oppression
of my people by the whites.

The man who delivered those words—
that man was a spear for the nation.

That man was prepared to die and did, in a sense,
though not senselessly by assassin or firing squad—

if anything, it must have been surreal to feel
one's body becoming rigid in symbolism as it does in death,

to witness your enemies give way to your exaltation
as hero for holding them to fire they deserved
but still, in so many ways, were spared.

I mean,   I know it would've killed me.
At least a little bit.
On the inside.

Inside the bronze that has
taken my widely recognizable shape.

It's Important I Remember
THAT I'M NOT BUILT FOR THIS FIGHT—

what little strength in my jawline I had left I lost
at the age of twenty-two, one year out of school,
living alone in Atlanta with a steady paycheck
and no appetite to meet anyone with a pulse.

I had a practice of picking up food from Krystal
after work: I would grab a few sliders, some fries,
sometimes topping them off with chili and cheese.
It was the closest thing to White Castle in the vicinity
when I got homesick. I did have a "castle," just as vacant
as Versailles was once they beheaded the monarch, but as
small as a matchbox, dingy carpet absorbing my hefty steps,
softening the blow of all that I am against the floor that is also,
I suppose, my neighbor's ceiling in life.
I'd certainly filled out with
the perks of relative riches for a person of my age. I was somewhere
between sad and comfortable, or perhaps commuted between the two
in the midsize sedan I'd signed my twenties away for, not even bothering
to walk that short distance into darkness.
In an earlier era, my flat feet
would've spared me from serving the empire overseas, but what happens
when it wages war on the people who I claim as my own? The suffering,
the sadism sets in: I speak against it, but my voice carries best down
the shaft of my own throat. I vote but can't collapse the ballot box to
think far enough outside this sham where white men concede only
to crueler white men.
I worried then and worry now that I'm
becoming more a coward, *becoming* implying change from one
state to another; and I indeed crossed state lines to come south—
as Lorraine Hansberry planned to before her life raisined—and
found out what kind of revolutionary I really was: a piercing
mind without a taste for gore, afraid in all ways ordinary and
thus useless in a time of urgency, which is always,
as far back or forward as these bloodshot eyes can
see.

It's Important I Remember

THAT FASCISM DIDN'T COME TO AMERICA, IT WAS ALREADY HERE—

wrapped in a flag and carrying a cross.

But the cross in question wasn't literal: In his hand was a Bible
turned upside down like the state device that martyred Saint Peter;
the flag was a black-and-white replica of the national
banner with a thin blue vein through the middle
like one that parts a brow between rage and reason.

There was tear gas deployed without a tear. There were
rubber bullets fired from weapons that also fire lethal rounds. There were
armored vehicles steering through the streets of the capital that stars our maps.

What we saw was only new to the people it was new to.
Some of us knew better. Been knew.

What the word is   to describe a J. Edgar Hoover.
What the word is   to describe a Eugene "Bull" Connor.
What the word is   to describe a Frank Rizzo or Richard J. Daley

from where we stand, where the leaves of grass brown and brittle.

Some of us *have* been to Wilmington, North Carolina, before,
where Air Jordan took flight from among other local luminaries
under very different, desperate circumstances—

sprinting from bullets, loose lumber, and ropes,
as their government, democratic and dark of hue, was tossed aside.

What the word is   for this begins softly enough in our mouths,
but that's not how it ends
as the teeth cut against it,
teeth that keep the record of who we were for forensics to later identify.

This is new to the people it's new to,
but some of us know better. Been known:

> If you ever see a black flock of birds scatter on the breeze,
> understand that the murders have started up again—

again	in the sense of	*active repetition.*
Repetition	in the sense of	*continuing practice.*
Practice	in the sense of	*attempting to perfect.*

It's Important I Remember

THAT GOOD ARTISTS COPY—

there was a good one, once, working in Vienna. No one
of transcendent talent. Nobody with a name deserving
to be spoken of in reverence. Ordinary as a lamppost,
blended into the background of the city like charcoal
beneath the finger pad, he sketched the movement
of the world passing him by in no detail glorious enough
that the Academy of Fine Arts saw fit to reward with
esteemed instruction. The artist then did as most artists do:
hustled in abject obscurity, bouncing between shelters,
trying to make scratch from oil paintings and watercolors.

There was a friendly Jewish man who purchased works
of his regularly, whose money fed the artist's needy body
as well as his tumorous sense of shame related to his
low social station and inability to articulate beauty,
his every creation characterized by coldness, lifelessness.

Shame followed the artist to Munich; it followed the artist
into the German army and Great War. Shame followed him
as if it were a whole other person prone to insecurity;
the shame swelled to unfathomable size like flames
engulfing an organ of democracy or a crowd with a fever.

He was a good artist, not a great one—not on canvas
and not on paper—but he had an eye that recognized
genius, knew where to search and where to send
his party's lawyers to retrieve the statutory stencils
to bring back and trace in the Reich, confident that
if it can happen in America, it can happen here.

It's Important I Remember

THAT THERE IS NO UNIVERSALLY RECOGNIZED DEFINITION—

but I prefer to theorize it as

empire pointing inward
or *gravity's pursuit of the sparrow.*

I tend to measure it

by the bloat of the city budget
and the boom it buys the cops to play with.

I often read about it

in books that I pulled from a trash can
fire in the park nearest my apartment.

The thread that holds a flag together.
An assembly line that makes dog whistles.
A light bulb over a brain dimmed on its right side.

It is impossible to write authoritatively about it
unless you are the authority and thus
have no intention to address what *it* is.

Violence without violins.
Truth as the shadow of the lie.
The monopoly on I.

Nobody agrees with me on the meaning
that wouldn't also argue particulars and process:

knowledge in the prison of a school;
God in the prison of a church;
citizen in the prison of a criminal.

You can never define a word outside a context,

and the life we are suffering is context
enough to say it, prior to it pronouncing itself
the only way it knows how, a hard way
allowing the lesson to be learned too late—

the loudest silence comes
after the loudest are silenced.

It's Important I Remember

THAT THE ENEMY OF MY ENEMY IS SOMEONE I DON'T KNOW VERY WELL—

not enough to confirm if our minds meet congruently
in their moral convictions,
circles drawn on the calendar in red to mark
the days of action we agreed to without uttering a word.

Rings around every square representing a unit of time—
Rome wasn't built in a day and didn't fall in one either, even if it should've.

Worthy accomplices see the forest and the trees
and the bodies hanging from their phantom limbs.

They know that we must
liberate everyone   everywhere   all at once.   Just this afternoon,

I told the animal rights advocate who solicited me for coin—
as police hurried a houseless person into invisibility across the street—

that a deficit of attention is a condition needing treatment,

and they didn't understand where my attitude was coming from
because they approached me
for having a kind face,
like a perfectly round balloon tied to the end of a stick.

If an unkindness is an assemblage of ravens, a kindness would be
one million faces like my own,
and there is only one of me.
There is only one of you.
And yet, we are hated by the same—
and yet, we are hated all the same,

though we are not the same   in the shape of our thinking,
or in our crimes against solidarity.

I can't call you   *friend*   while you withhold your forgiveness.
You can't call me   *friend*   while not extending an apology.

But my enemy, who
is your enemy, bitterly,
calls you *dead* and me *buried*,

without even a stone gummed in the dirt like a tooth to identify me.

~~01.27.2017~~

pledges of allegiance

It's Important I Remember

THAT HARRY S. TRUMAN WAS PRESENTED WITH FOUR OPTIONS—

dropping the atomic bomb on Japan was only one of them.

Rather than the big bomb, the president could've chosen to
rain fire with smaller shells over a wider swath of the country.

Rather than the big bomb, the president could've chosen to
land the troops on shore and sweep from city to city,
town to town, fighting trained soldiers
and civilians armed with crude weapons and will.

Rather than the big bomb, the president could've chosen—
the big bomb, but steered it to an island without any settlements
to scare Japan into surrender as their brass took in the mushroom cloud
through binoculars a safe distance away.

In weighing options, conversion between metrics gets complicated
and the president—*this* president—was a simple man:

War requires that one life and one life do not equal.

The president, with his advisors, reviewed the maps
and marked the targets—Hiroshima, Nagasaki—
for their military relevance and for the fact their buildings hadn't
been toppled yet, meaning the bomb's might would be without doubt.

The day Nagasaki disappeared, three days after Hiroshima
dissolved into dust, President Truman returned correspondence
to Reverend Samuel McCrea Cavert, who had pleaded
for the bombing to cease: *When you have to deal with a beast,*
you have to treat him as a beast.

The Manhattan Project, which produced the atomic bombs
for the United States, cost $2.2 billion dollars to bring
to its expected conclusion. Two bombs leveled two cities
and brought the largest armed conflict in history to a close.

A dozen American prisoners of war died to do so, in Hiroshima,
but in yet another miracle of Western ingenuity,
no additional human lives were lost.

It's Important I Remember

THAT THE UNITED STATES HASN'T ISSUED A DECLARATION OF WAR SINCE WORLD WAR II—

so when the sun rose evangelically the next day,
on Wednesday, there was no way to exactly explain
the state of mind or what held the State itself intact.

The morning prior, *nonstate actors* committed
the crime of the new century, converted commercial
airliners into analogues of guided missiles. Aero-
phobia swiftly overcame the population, even me, who
as a little boy committed playtime to jet plane models,
never pretending anything other than a smooth landing.

That would've been enough panic, but it didn't stop there—
the air currents that cool hot heads moved into the past
tense; the silence settled in; the fear became increasingly
dangerous for lacking the specificity of familiar landmarks.

The people couldn't point to al-Qaeda on a map, so the people
pointed everywhere; every border collapsed except those of
our bodies, which were subject, not sovereign. In the weeks
after the attacks, many of us slept through the night with
American flags over our icy bones as comforters, not thinking
this a premonition of decades of dead soldiers to follow.

While the adults followed the news minute by minute, riling
themselves up to retaliate, I tailed brown kids through school
halls like shade cast in human shape, tallied them outnumbered
like I was, the mass of students suddenly aware of what Muslims
"look like" swelling to great size, swayed by a sensational media.

I knew when Nader referred to himself as a sand nigger
in my presence, casually, it was his way of dapping up.
When Jeet never came outside, I figured it was to avoid
confusion around country of origin. Nisreen's people
didn't even have a country, but there was no point in

saying that aloud, not when the second President Bush had given his generals the green light, their latitude and longitude limitless in the legislative terms set by Congress.

World War II was the last war the United States won and the last it fought by letter: We must call what came afterward another name. We await words for what we're living through to be born, to help put death to the death.

It's Important I Remember

THAT THEY HATE US FOR OUR FREEDOM—

but not for our option to worship a higher power or praise none,
          on paper;

and not for the frequency with which we pull back
the tab on a lukewarm can of Natural Light;

but not for the unsanctioned self-expression we're permitted,
          on paper;

and not for the red line we draw, aside from Chicagoans,
down the length of an Oscar Mayer wiener;

but not for the chance to draw our leaders like straws from the lot of us
without regard to parentage,
          on paper;

and not for the raucous swirl we fill the bowl
of a football stadium with on weekends;

but not for our allowance to assemble of one purpose in one place,
          on paper;

and not for the practice of calling our winning ball clubs *world* champions;

          they hate us for, if anything,

folding that fabled parchment into an airplane
that drops the most difficult truths overseas,
over foreign cities, jungles, and sands: knowledge
heavy enough to kill on impact if one lets it
weigh on them—that hate *can* be rational. And if

there *is* hate there, they hate the US, which
doesn't translate to the American people per se,
but try convincing flag-waving patriots otherwise

and you will fail.

You will be just
another quagmire in nation building

while what document deems that we're free dissolves
in our pooled bloodthirst like tissue—paper—
until the US is us, and we are it, plural as the number one.

It's Important I Remember

THAT AMERICA IS FULL OF SHIT—

not quite literally, but nearly. I mean,
how much time do you have for a history?

Just hear me out: American imperialism
was built on bird shit. And, yes, I recognize

our empire offshoots from the British one,
broke loose and overran nation after nation
of Indigenous peoples who lived on

most visibly as the logos of our professional
franchises or collegiate clubs playing sports
that embrace collision and spectacle.

This is the part you're passingly aware of,
what we dress with turkey and stuffing every year
to aid digestion of the despicable.

The bird poop is more historically amusing,
though the same kind of terrible.

Before the Civil War was raging,
farmlands needed nourishment
after settler karma had fully set into the soil;

to increase yield, yeomen looked for fertilizer,
for guano, the scat of seabirds built up
over eons in enormous quantities on islands
scattered around the Caribbean and Pacific.

Rather than deal with the Peruvians,
who controlled the bulk of the trade,

Americans pushed off to guano islands
and grabbed those, one by one,

when no people were already
present—put their literal flagpoles
in the dookie rock and everything.

Because of that, and the spats
with foreign guano miners that followed,
Congress passed legislation in 1856

that named these types of islands legally
American territory upon enterprise's petition.

But this didn't settle the matter
even if it settled the land
with workmen and manual tools.

What brought the country closer to fever
pitch on imperialism was, inadvertently,
some brothers from Baltimore who rose up

on a tiny dot known as Navassa that the US
didn't want black-ass Haiti to have dominion over.

Inside that historical irony was the iron
will of those black workers to refuse subjection
to the cruelty of their white overseers, a rebuff

to breaking their backs for broken promises
and extracting from the land as company policy
extracted from their famished pockets.

Five white men died in labor's revolt.
The workers were cuffed, charged, convicted,

then freighted back to Baltimore like cargo,
with, again, a dark tinge of irony.

Luckily, there were some lawyers
more or less waiting for them at the dock,
three black and three white.

They argued before the courts, on behalf
of the black workers, that their convictions
were unconstitutional, that US law

had no jurisdiction, being that Navassa
was not part of the United States.

My no-longer-Negro self finds it funny
that *Navassa* ends like *massa* on paper,
but that emphasizes the whole damn point:

The high court upheld the American
land claim under law I cited previously,

kept the sentences for murder unrevised,
and left those black men waiting on death row

until President Benjamin Harrison
commuted the men to imprisonment
and lifetime labor. Again, ironic.

That went down back in 1891, already
thirty-five years deep into the bird shit.

The Spanish-American War followed
seven years later, and relatedly came

Cuba, Puerto Rico, the Philippines, Hawaii,
and a host of "unincorporated territories"

with titles that evoke tropical vacations,
all legalized in our jurisprudence alone.

We don't mine for droppings anymore,
now that we mix our own compounds;

flocks don't fly between the little islands
like they did before the days of dynamite
disrupted their migration patterns—

but their old routes are still flown
by US aircraft returning to base.

It turns out that when a pilot playfully
flips the bird to their fellow
service members in the mess hall,

they're making light of what
they're actually doing on active duty.

It's Important I Remember

THAT THE ENEMY IS ALWAYS WITHIN—

it had never been more evident to me than that night.

In the evening, I slid over to the main library to visit her
while I knew she was on the clock for work study.
Exams were coming up anyway, so I thought: *Why learn*
a lesson alone when you can learn it with someone.

Hours earlier, helicopter blades sliced the black sky
above Abbottabad into fabric fit for funeral attire
with gunfire folded into the creases of the night.

For God and country—
so swore the Navy SEAL to his distant commander
watching from an electronic eagle eye.

When American Airlines Flight 77 breached
one of the five faces of the Pentagon,
my classmate's uncle was killed:
That boy's name was Luke, a biblical title.

Holy war had come to our one nation under God,
as we pledge it to be in our classrooms, *the* one nation,
as we believe it to be in our hearts, and everyone
around me fell under the spell of a medieval impulse.

To that point, there hadn't been enough blood
to wash away the curse that overcame my country
because it wasn't *his* blood—until the day it was,
the headlines in bold like memorial wall engravings.

We were in the digital media center when the news
broke us. As the shock shook off, she and I
popped open my laptop and waited
for the president's late-night broadcast to stream.

He said what one would expect
a president of the United States to say
when a page in history turns.

I didn't linger on what his words were but on
how he walked: a solemn yet unmistakable swagger
in his bouncing shoulders, not a speck of dirt on them.

It was cool *or* it was chilling.
          Or it was cool *because* it was chilling.
                    Or it was chilling because it *was*
cool, I hated to admit
to myself, discomforted by my own quietude.

I pushed the screen down and panned the scene
like a device with an aperture designed to intake epiphany.

I've opted to mute the footage in my mental archives:
Everyone's smiles were already in stereo; their teeth were
so loud—as loud as the world always says we Americans are,
or how I imagine bombs must be when killing the innocent.

It's Important I Remember

THAT EXILE DOESN'T PROMISE EXTRICATION—

the life of James Baldwin, as in so many other ways,
is instructive on this matter. In 1986, a year prior to the period
of his final sentence, he addressed the National Press Club in DC,
simplifying an anguish that kept him among the living as much
as it nearly ended his life on multiple occasions: *I was getting out*
of here. I didn't so much go to Paris as leave New York,
with forty bucks in his pocket and not even enough French
to lick a postage stamp. Before he boarded that airplane,
there had been disturbances that stirred the ink that stirred the world.
Eugene Worth, loved, maybe beloved though unconfessed, shot the gap
between the George Washington Bridge and the Hudson River
with the speed of a cannonball, splashing grief against James's
singular eyes, the joyous signature of his lips. The disrespects had
been as rampant as they were ordinary, the prospects of life in Harlem
as grim as Baldwin was black. Before he was no one's Negro, he
was everybody's nigger, and rather than break under that burden,
he decided to break away to France and found that the City of Lights
was not lit up by burning crosses, that his American origin made him
no serious threat while strolling along the Seine but, instead, a fascination
admired at a distance like artwork in the galleries of the Louvre; he was
mostly unbothered, in a foreign turn, save for the short stint in jail on a false
charge of stealing levied against a man whose descent from stolen people
separated him, psychically, from the Africans he met while living in exile.

The relative peace he moved with in Paris was uncomfortable and therefore
no peace at all. The translation of *nigger* into French was not a civilian's word
but a phrase in the language of the State: Algerians, exceedingly poor but
proud and percolating, were bloodied in the streets, stuffed in the prisons,
tossed soundlessly into the serenaded river from bridges that vehicles drive
and legs walk. *Liberty*, *equality*, *fraternity*: There it was to see so clearly
as with an eagle's bald pupils. It was a brutality one could live in, cozy and
familiar—with paper and pen for novels, plays, and essays—a banner of red
and white and blue flying atop the famous tower under which lovers kiss.

It's Important I Remember

THAT PALESTINIANS KNOW OUR POLICE BETTER THAN WE DO—

know who many of us, at times, refer to as *po-po* or *five-o*
or *twelve*. Palestinians refer to them as *voyeurs*, as *trainees*
come to the Holy Land to learn the arts of surveillance, crowd
control, and use of force from deputies graded out as savants.

Heaven has a ghetto in Gaza; Jesus of Nazareth was executed
by the authorities in the West Bank once upon a Gospel, after
Judas Iscariot snitched about his whereabouts for silver. Where
the natives live, boys become men if they're lucky—otherwise, they

grow up to be ghosts their siblings wish would rise again in flesh,
as Deja and them did when Mike Brown was put down by the cop
like a gorilla that discovered the delight of smiling. The city rose
up from the concrete in a bloom of boom, fires everywhere,

little ballads of rage riffing on Baldwin's prescient writings.
911 dialed 9/11 and tactical units swarmed peopled streets
as though an army meeting foreign adversaries at the border
of the idea of a nation, building fences with their bodies—

shields up, helmets on, masks ready—not sparing property
our anger as action so much as putting a safe space between
themselves and what they deserved from those they swear at
rather than protect. They served us the gas of grief and wailing,

cannister after cannister, that only folks half a world from Ferguson
could teach us how to cope with as our bodies tried coughing up
our very souls and American lies scorched the linings of our lungs.
They tweeted advice to us from a prison with a view of a teasing sea

that many of our countryfolk, on this side of the same cruel coin,
pay a pretty penny to vacation unaware of the poems we're passing
to one another that would be contraband in hell, as Assata attests—
what we wrote with quills plucked from pigeons because the doves

fell dead from the sky darkened by ash and bad intentions, packed to the horizon with helicopters turning circles to stay above us, keeping watch as well as station close to the throne of God, the creator we share with our adversaries like lands those of us engaged in struggle know nothing beyond.

~~08.20.1619~~

property's rights

It's Important I Remember

THAT HISTORY IS ALL A BIG MISUNDERSTANDING—

he took a wrong turn and so did the world, I figure;
couldn't even find a real Illini around me growing up

but I obviously know why. Because of him

the Spanish came, the Portuguese, the French, the English, the Dutch;
they brought smallpox and measles with them, brought the horses

and the guns the Native nations used against the cowboy
protagonists in all those fifties Westerns. Meanwhile the white folks

got potatoes, sunflowers, chocolate; meanwhile
the white folks got some chocolate-

colored peoples to come by compulsion

and this is how my family came to walk across the pages
of your textbooks, chained in line and hunched toward the ground

like distant ancestors to humankind and not men
and women and children. It's all been uphill from there

and I'm winded, holding my howling knees, barely standing
against the steep slope of some pyramid scheme called

progress, laughing at the expression *winds of change*.
What comedy that is—I've got nothing at my back

except a boot, my belly and cheek made raw against the sandpaper
of the sidewalk. I could honestly go to sleep right here,

as easily as the boy I used to be would. I could be the most
obscure footnote in the records or, if this world were even

remotely fair, I could be great.

It's Important I Remember
THAT THOMAS JEFFERSON WAS A RAPIST—

period. That's fact as much as
what's etched in expensive stone:

Here was buried Thomas Jefferson
Author of the Declaration of American Independence
of the Statute of Virginia for Religious Freedom
and Father of the University of Virginia.

Father of other entities as well, I must add:
human properties whose descendants can
still feel his intrusions where their molars socket.

Ache in the gums can easily dissuade
people from speaking, even if
they have an importance to voice. She,
in her peculiar station, could either say *yes,*
master, or she could say nothing at all.

Sally was not a love story but a long story,
she herself harvested from the same violence
he pleasurably slipped inside her to mother.

No matter her complexion under candlelight,
the shadow she casts over Monticello
is dark enough for epithet.

In starless hours, when only indecency happens,
he slowly slid her into position like furniture,
which she was, something to shift the weights
of his life onto, he, the intellectual revolutionary,
the devoted statesman, the pitiful widower.

When he whispered *this is mine* in her ear,
he meant it how neither man nor law ever should;
the only thing she should've done, she did—

again and again and again, *yes*.

It's Important I Remember

THAT ENSLAVED PEOPLE MARRIED HERE—

scaled the summit of ovation in one leap
over that solemn broom; swept demons
away; were swept up and into a scheme
of tender mercies, salve for souls frayed
like a singular allowance of cloth
by field labor under sun and overseer.
In those days, if death parted you
from your beloved, then *you*
were blessed beyond belief
being that license for the ceremony was
recorded on a cloud that came close
enough to the earth to stain with fingertips.

When he parted you,   you were parted.

When the white man of white men
spoke the words it was
as if the continents split,
the countenance split,
an ocean's worth of salt water spilled
into every sort of separation
now surfacing on the human face:
a man's, a woman's, a child's
like both and like neither.
But one point to make
in favor of advancement
is that we can say goodbye
on our own terms now,
on good terms or bad,
though you and I hold out hope
that our magical evening will be
when the shaky ground beneath us
is reconciled for good
like the broken bond of a bone.

Contracts have been signed,
checks have been cut and hard-
earned cash withdrawn
damn near out of my ice-cold hands:
All that's left is to vow
continuance in the face
of every conflict and
challenge that confronts us,
contorts us into knots inside
that mock the one we tied before God.

Love, I'm as hefty as a sparrow can be
and still be able to defy the law of gravity,
soaring at the prospect of a promise,
the dress I haven't laid eyes on delicately
resting in a garment box in our closet
next to the clutter of modern domesticity.
I'm reflecting on all the bygone
that I favor phenotypically when your own
father's face crosses my mind like
analog noise and I anxiously twist
my finger where a precious band is
soon to be, easing back into the heaven
we purchased on sale from West Elm
and turning on the TV—cable news—
the white man of white men on-screen
where I left him the night before
every night for years now.

When he parts you, *you are parted.*

That's what all the journalists say,
partly why some friends claim kids
would be a particularly irrational decision.
Yet I've insisted. And we've decided
on first names even if not a firm number,

as we are descendants of dreamers
who never saw black as black. We—
an abundance they feared and abhorred.
I love you, in light of that dark past,
is so insufficient, so light
on how we save each other each day,
but it's all that I have to say:
This is my singular allowance,
a simple sleeve to wear on
what might be called feelings
but more faithfully should be called
faith.

It's Important I Remember

THAT ABRAHAM LINCOLN ALWAYS MEASURED BEFORE HE CUT—

saying less, for now, about the steady hand holding the pen
of proclamation and presidential address, saying more

of the one wrapped around the axe handle,
that brought the head down straight and split the rails

that built the fence that became the border
that separated the "civilized" from those they labeled *savage*

and created farmland from their land, which Abe labored on
for no payment except for his father's admonishment

while living on the frontier of difficult feelings, eyes forever full
of mood and storm. Say more of the man of lithe stature who was

too small in status to perjure himself before the public, of the candidate
who was common enough to be a trustworthy steward over

the common interest as far as working men saw it. Say more
of the sense of duty and command he had, of his executive competence

and sense of determination. See, I can indulge a good myth
made of a mortal man up until the point it makes myth of me as well:

when my thanks are invited implicitly in every retelling of his story
for a piece of paper that cut around electoral edges, that freed

my forebears as battle tactic to spare a fiction grand enough
for people to keep dying for in perpetuity. He would save the Union

without freeing any slave if he could, the president wrote
to Horace Greeley with hallmark honesty: Without any slaves,

it wouldn't have been possible to save it, and without any slaves,
it wouldn't have needed saving, the war between states and their stated

ideals made moot, so say more of the price paid to refortify the foundation
of a house that is burning now because it didn't fall back then. Say more

on prudence when insistence is the only righteous option. Say more
about what happens when common men have a measure of control

in their leathered hands: ink and parchment, blade and hilt.

It's Important I Remember

THAT THE FINAL SCENE IN *DJANGO UNCHAINED* IS THE DESTRUCTION OF CANDYLAND—

cathartic, if I can say that
about the letting of so much blood.

I cackled. I clapped. I consumed the ice-cold

Coca-Cola while Django exacted sweet vengeance
wearing round shades and a purple jacket like Prince—

well, burgundy—firing off his trusty six-shooter,
slotting a bullet for every letter in *nigger*,

the loudest word in the film if not the most used,

as much the writer's fetish creeping into the script
as it was a signifier of the time period

and also, I think, thematically appropriate

seeing as one white man put that word in
another white man's mouth to begin with so long ago.

That's how we've gotten to this point in the story:
2013, nearly a year since Trayvon wasn't here anymore.

At times it feels that all we're doing is living
through somebody else's motion picture, that we're

narrative sacrifices for some convoluted redemption arc,

so it's hard not to relish the rare scene you actually want
to act out, busting caps in all their racist asses,

blowing up the big house with sticks of dynamite
and riding out on horseback with Kerry Washington,

the only problem being you still had to play a slave
to get there. But, in the end, that's nothing new:

That's just history.

It's Important I Remember

THAT JOHN BROWN WAS THE FIRST PERSON EXECUTED FOR TREASON IN US HISTORY—

tried and convicted by the Commonwealth of Virginia
on this and two other grave charges:

one, conspiring with slaves to incite insurrection;
two, murder—all three stemming from his raid on Harpers Ferry.

There was no doubt of Brown's guilt based upon
state law and the evidentiary support presented,

including a provisional constitution he penned
at Frederick Douglass's house that would abolish slavery.

As Brown's body dangled lifeless from the gallows,
a stage actor watched with unwavering fascination,

finding solace in the death of an enemy to his beloved country
but also enamored by said enemy's undeniable bravery.

In just over five years' time, that same thespian,
John Wilkes Booth, would assassinate the American president

who most directly brought upon the end of chattel slavery here
before himself being shot dead in a barn two weeks later: a fugitive.

Of the two Johns terminated by state power, the traitor is
determined by what you believe this country of ours to truly be:

the one born of the Declaration of Independence or
the one born of the Declaration of Independence;

where the border is drawn around the word

men,
all ~~beings~~ things being equal.

~~06.17.2021~~

justice delayed is justice denied

It's Important I Remember

THAT TONI MORRISON DUBBED BILL CLINTON THE FIRST BLACK PRESIDENT—

which I wonder if she ended up wanting to take back
as surely as the first statement has been taken out of context
by every nineties black stand-up act you could name,

a silly notion suspended in a white void unaffiliated to the raw
feeling of melanin at the essence of Morrison

penning that the forty-second president of the United States,
impeached, was being *metaphorically*
seized and body-searched. Yes, we got the sax solo

on *Arsenio* and also *I didn't like it and didn't inhale*
as if, with instinctive deftness, that's the distinction between us

and them when you get right down to it—
having discipline versus needing it imposed—
that indelible smirk I can't help but see

traced by the slim, shadowed crease of a pillowcase hood,
good ol' Slick Willie rolling a doobie with congressional bills,

Otis Redding rolling over in his grave
whenever somebody said, *That white boy from Hope*
got soul, just needed a little ass is all,

as all the prisons of this nation swelled with the phatness
of our bodies, stripped bare of context like poor ideas
and birdcaged by popular vote and demand,

nobody, I tell you, nobody getting off
outside White House walls, that international players monument

to free labor. All that laissez-faire commentary
being broadcasted is never balanced or fair, just lazy.

It will kill you if you don't pull a loaded question on it, my brother:
You'll find a cloudy stain on a solid blue dress
and think the sky has fallen

and you wouldn't be wrong in the slightest,
but you would be a sucker, sorry to say.

It's Important I Remember

THAT ORANGE IS THE NEW BLACK—

and, in the end, I'm of one mind on this.

The smartest call the *Orange* showrunners ever made was reducing
Piper's screen time. A satisfying story would never be about her,
not because a person of her profile is some stranger to crime,
but because they are, more so, a stranger to punishment.

Taystee, though, was my girl, an everygirl from around the way
braided into predicament in a tale that tatters the viewer's heart.

That describes, by and large, the backstories of the colorful cast:
black stories and lack stories.

There are so many wrong places— *wronged* places—
to originate from in the land of almond milk and raw honey.

Time doesn't sit at ninety-degree angles in South Central Los Angeles,
for example. Some kids don't get to be seen as angels, even in death.

Black slims you to nothingness and that's why it's forever
fashionable, the classic choice, institutionalized.

Where the show title's popular phrase comes from is the
reality of language as the system that the system uses. *New*
implies there's a prior or previous—not in captivity's complexion,
which is the sociological constant, but in method— an *old* way.

Michelle Alexander writes the N-word on her legal pad
and underlines it, understanding the words of the phrase change
while the structure of the sentence doesn't.

In 1865, the Thirteenth Amendment abolished slavery
and involuntary servitude except as punishment for a crime.

The first popular adjustable handcuffs
were made in 1865.

National Handcuff Day is celebrated in the United States
during February every year.

These sentences will never change,

nor that the skin of an orange jumpsuit peels from the body like rind
while the skin beneath the jumpsuit doesn't.

It's Important I Remember

THAT JOURNALISM IS THE FIRST DRAFT OF HISTORY—

and Ida B. Wells, well, frustrated
the engenderment of the official record;

crisscrossed the country interviewing
poplars that had been accessories to atrocities,

not unlike that which felled her dear friend
Thomas Moss in Memphis, what became the lynch-

pin to her crusade, though he specifically
never dangled from a wooden limb

like natural confections scanned for bruises
in the produce section of People's Grocery.

There is no justice here, he's believed
to have said before being proven

correct, after the mob descended on his jail cell
with cocked weapons, wearing black masks, blacker

even than those that frame ivory teeth trained
to curvature by the terror of sudden swings

in white men's temperament: teeth, it was told
around town after town, that rot from the sugar

of white women, sugar that black men steal,
which makes the bloodshed that much sweeter,

worth snapping necks for, like stalks of sugarcane,
to say nothing of the black women left hanging at all.

The big lie looms large over the ripening fruits,
standing on their porches with shotguns loaded—

or with their luggage packed, prepared to spread wing
and fly before they're flown up the bark of a tree

with hounds nipping at their heels and bulbs flashing
for the morning newspapers where it would read

that a dangerous deviant was sentenced to death
by a coalition of concerned citizens: a red record

printed authoritatively in black until a black woman—
Ida B.—took her proverbial red pen to the horrid story

and made history retract its initial word on the subject,
though not its inherent threat, which is set in tombstone.

It's Important I Remember

THAT NINA SIMONE WROTE "MISSISSIPPI GODDAM" IN LESS THAN ONE HOUR—

and she meant every word.

At times the lyric is insistent, an immaculate conception,
which is to say, perhaps, that urgency is the one true God we answer to

and God, truly, is the one thing we need urgently:

Medgar was dead from a bullet in the back.
Four little beauties in Birmingham.

The record was put to wax at Carnegie Hall in New York City,
a spotlight on the singer as round and hot as the sun
that oversaw a boy's body bob up from the Tallahatchie.

In grief and despair,
it is the soul that is heavy and the bones that are weightless;

Ms. Simone bore her soul, birthed a song that was more than song,
laid the brunt of blackness on thin waves of air.

When Philips Records sent the single to radio stations across the nation,
some were returned with the vinyl broken cleanly in half;

I've long wondered if that partition was premeditated,
hateful vandalism of the voice,

or if it was a moment of art imitating life so precisely
that the 45s themselves, sometime during transport,

had become Nina's heart.

It's Important I Remember

THAT THE MORAL ARC OF THE UNIVERSE BENDS—

but it doesn't break, and neither breaks toward justice
nor away from it. It simply bends, as the bow does
before propelling the arrow where it may, agnostic
to everything but flight. I don't mean to make morality
a weapon in this way, but it already is one and has been
for some time. The shackles, after all, were explained
as saving us from ourselves, our naked savagery,
though it was their whip that licked us and left a kind
of tactile text on our bodies. The Bible will have a man
beating on someone as easily as it will have another
taking one, turning the other cheek, civilly disobedient
even when the bombs blow up in their church, not to say
saying no to violence isn't commendable, just to say
a strong case can be made for cracking a skull or two
like an everyday egg in hopes whatever golden light
resides inside shines through, throughs the crimson tide
for the rest of time so the tide will, mercifully, recede.

It's Important I Remember

THAT AMERICA EXISTS BY A KIND OF GRACE—

free and unmerited favor.
I swear to God

this is what I'll tell my sweet children should she and I be blessed with
such an overwhelming responsibility as taking custody of small futures.

I can fathom them only by intuition, not by touch. They're not ghouls but
haunt me amiably, branched—through their mother's father's mother—

from the Pilgrim landing at Plymouth Rock, which then became the rock
that landed on the balance of their relatives on the other side of history:

the poor souls who shivered while shackled in ship bellies, whose faces
ripple across my eyes' dark and troubled waters in moments of reflection.

That my kids' bodies refuse fissure where their frictions most happen—
joints, borders of motion—hints poetically that this nation may find peace

through movements of people, give restoratively for what it took ruthlessly.
The thieving of land from some begot the thieving of freedom from others

begot a mighty stream that hasn't ceased flowing into the gulf of our concern
for one another, our differences permanently stained by blood and cabernet.

I wouldn't be a worthwhile father if I spared them all the bloody details:
the *t*'s crossed and burned on lawns, *i*'s dotted by bullets. I'll tell them

in Jamestown,
the devil lived;
the devil lived;
in Tippecanoe,
in Gnadenhutten,
the devil lived;

in Round Valley,
the devil lived;
the devil lived;
in Sand Creek,
in Mankato,
the devil lived;

in Memphis,
the devil lived;
the devil lived;
in Opelousas,
in New Orleans,
the devil lived;

in Skeleton Cave,
the devil lived;
the devil lived;
in Vicksburg,
in Colfax,
the devil lived;

in Clinton,
the devil lived;
the devil lived;
in Bear River,
in Rock Springs,
the devil lived;

in Hamburg,
the devil lived;
the devil lived;
in Wounded Knee,
in Thibodaux,
the devil lived;

in Wilmington,
the devil lived;
the devil lived;
in Slocum,
in Springfield,
the devil lived;

in Porvenir,
the devil lived;
the devil lived;
in Elaine,
in Chicago,
the devil lived;

in Ocoee,
the devil lived;
the devil lived;
in Rosewood,
in Tulsa,
the devil lived;

in Charleston,
the devil lived;
the devil lived;
in Washington, DC,
in El Paso,
the devil live—

I have full faith they'll understand me. My brood won't be delicate
but deliberate, unflappable. I won't allow them to know me as a liar:

They'll recognize early on that lies get our kind killed.

I see it now: We're driving down 71st Street in a minivan as I once did
with my parents, the road dedicated to a boy who once lived near here

and died so much closer to home, in a sense. Maybe my kids will also
whistle when they're anxious or scared half to ghost, will instinctively

comprehend the many means death has of making contact with us like
an old classmate, or coworker, or neighbor you waved at from the porch

like a flag awaiting visit of rain.

This is the home of the brave, I'll sing

to my darlings before every kickoff and tip-off, honoring our own little
house built on a hill where a hall light shines always but there's no TEC

on the dresser, no shotgun on the back seat of the car, no revolver tucked
behind the toilet tank with duct tape. We do scare, yes, but only scare

so easily. We've seen it all before we've even seen anything, have sight
in color before sight in color. Doctorates only recently started studying

how trauma travels between two points on a line of succession without
losing one bit of intensity: the blues chord vibrating in our black matters.

Here's what a scar is: being capable of spelling *Mississippi* and yet
unable to speak it aloud at all; answering to the name your instructor

won't mispronounce but never what they call you where your parents
come from; drinking yourself to dust out on the rez as sun boils sand.

It's hard to get over harm that you had no choice but to make a home in;
Old Glory's stripes must signify the flow of a wound over pale knuckles.

The distinction between that banner and the one I hope never to become
is it being an act of mercy to fly me upside down, not disrespect. Mercy

is why that star-spangled banner yet waves, why no mob has burned down
the White House since the redcoats did back in 1814—it's far too painful

to destroy what you've created even when it attempts to destroy you first.
Ask God about God's children. Ask us about you, after the funerals return

earth to earth. Grief, I know, can shape itself an open hand or a handgun:
Which possibility can we no longer afford?

The end of forgiveness
is the end of everything. The end of forgiveness
is the end of everything. The end of forgiveness
is the end of everything. The end of forgiveness
is the end of everything. The end of forgiveness
is the end of everything. The end of forgiveness
is the end of everything. The end of forgiveness
is the end of everything—

this is what I'll tell them, my beautiful babies,
and then they'll tell me, verb above verbiage,

what that really means.
How sweet the feeling.

~~05.25.2020~~

the opposite of love

It's Important I Remember

THAT A CURRENT EVENT IS A CURRENT—

carries a charge, attracts the opposition's glee   or anger
to the anonymous comment section.   Of course, the current

state of affairs flows through me entirely,   twists static
into my hair: To say 60 percent of body weight is water

is to say I'm especially sensitive   to the latest scandalous
headline, not shocked in the least but   an electric field

of hard feelings,   repelling people regardless of intention.
My connection to the world is   loosening by the second.

The things I should be wired tightly to   my grip has
been softening on since they killed him   the first time.

I could burn a house down in seconds   with the wrong
spark, with ease.   Someone like me happens every day.

My country is a house divided against itself   so perhaps
that is the one to go up in smoke   when a housewife

tries to toast   a slice of whole-grain bread in the suburbs.
What a shame that would be,   what a quiet misfortune:

All anybody would've needed to do   was check on me
once in a white moon,   give me a good hope to hold

on to again. The fix seems so easy and yet   the concern
so far from mind.   The American dream has long been

to own a home that you must   *maintain*, therefore you
own this catastrophe   waiting to happen in the wall,

the thing you never knew you were   wishing for: me,
aflame, bringing it all down   to where I feel most days.

It's Important I Remember

THAT HISTORY DOESN'T REPEAT, IT RHYMES—

for example, President Abraham Lincoln

had a secretary named Kennedy

and President John F. Kennedy

had a secretary named Lincoln.

Okay, okay . . .

that hasn't ever been verified on Abe's end,

but that's not the rhyme anyway.

You already know the bullet is the rhyme

between those two, the opening it made

in the mind for grieving that is both unique

and reminiscent. Rhyme, in essence,

is the repetition of one root sound,

potting it in new grammar.

A fresh rhyme refreshes the spirit,

tickles the lips into an upturn,

but history is, like, the laziest rapper ever, I swear.

History rhymes *violence* with *violins* and calls it a fucking day.

History rhymes *nigga* with *nigga* except

does it using the OG version

of that word, which anchors

the ole lynching tree to stolen land.

Here's the slant heard in the timeline:

It's September 23, 2020, and that same damn word reverberates
through the happenings of the afternoon news—a black woman
shot to death in her own home by Louisville police six months ago
and the single charge the grand jury brought forward against only
one officer out of the group is first-degree wanton endangerment
clicking three times off the judge's tongue. Lazy. Lacking
any allusion to the extinguishment of Breonna's beautiful life,
finding more concern for her white neighbors next door and the holes
in their wall needing spackling paste. And the reference history pulls
into its tired rap isn't pop as in crossover, it's pompous, a gloat
nothing less than grotesque: *If we hadn't stopped to drink pop,*
it wouldn't have taken that long. That was also September 23,
but back in 1955, when a jury in Mississippi acquitted murderers
and clanged glass bottles of Coke over Emmett Till's mangled body,
a boy, black and mild, who got lied on by somebody's white neighbor.

Look: Today is our first time here,
but we've been here before.

I've been *here* before.

I hear it with my heart, yes—

and it sounds—

it sounds—

sounds—

so devastatingly wack.

Devastatingly.

It's Important I Remember

THAT MY EMPLOYER CARES ABOUT MY SAFETY AND WELL-BEING—

there's a disturbance in the police force
in proximity to my assigned office:

Protesters are anticipated to assemble
in Times Square at 7:00 P.M.,
and it is critical that I receive this

civil unrest information.

I'm advised to sign up for mobile alerts
and follow the instructions
of local authorities during this

potential life safety event.

Reach out to Global Security Operations at ______________.
Reach out to People Experience at ______________.

Reach out to your manager for support,
the message tells me, among other specific details,

like who the demonstration organizers are
or that the body cam footage will be released in Memphis
one hour prior to start time.

The automated system is not equipped with enough
EQ to account for what my people experience
in proximity to my assigned office every single day;

in this manner, I know that
artificial intelligence is already a match
for most of the individuals I meet.

I don't find security in this, but the familiar,
at times, can approximate safety
or comfort you when you're exhausted

from working, or worrying over
whatever you want to call this life
event that almost feels like
                                        an eventuality.

It's Important I Remember

THAT WE'RE NOT BEARING WITNESS, WE'RE WATCHING—

which I will attempt to explain, but first
I must find my smartphone.

I feel as naked without it as my clothes must without me
in them providing shape and structure.
                                                            iPhone. Android:

the way it pulses in my pocket after a stimulus signals in,
how it holds and withholds so many words within
its hard casing, the ability to focus on the subject it possesses

leads me along like the figurative heart by its whims or intuitions;
it enraptures the soul or, perhaps, ensnares it, digitizes
said ephemeral entity that ballads are born from in bytes of data.

        Like Osiris, I'm stored in so many pieces in so many places;
        like that god of the underworld, the judge of the dead,

        I will be murdered by my brother, by which I mean
        someone with at least one association we share
        even if we do not wish we shared it.

These days, I'm not sure we feel the same way
so much as a share of one feeling split millions of ways
into a twitch above the eye—

you and I phone and droid, seeing but lacking in-
sight—which is likely why

the legs don't get the signal and the hands
don't get the signal and the moment overwhelms us
because it is too much data to process for what
we've been compressed to by the scale of devastation

except in that instant when we finally wiggle the phone free
from our pocket and point it at the crime—

though not in accusation,
as devices can't do that, only a person,

and there isn't one
anymore.

It's Important I Remember

THAT IN ORDER FOR WHITE PEOPLE TO STUDY MY LIFE, THEY MUST FIRST STUDY MY BODY—

once my muscles harden in a manner I'd have hoped for
as a teen thinking it would dissuade death from trying me,
they will slip their fingers into every opening they can find
still wet with young wine and take pleasure in knowing this
is not a body that belonged to a real man. And though not
what they'd call woman either, written in cursive or calculus,
it is undoubtedly some woman's body of work—mother, sister,
lover—tossed hastily in the trash bag. Cause of death: the usual.
Time of death: on time, like an act of God. Local press is present
just outside the operating room doors with only the most pertinent
questions for those people with the untold shame of loving who
the body used to be.
How poor were his grades in grammar school?
Did he smoke weed or just sell it? On a scale of fast to insanely fast,
at what speed did he veer toward violence?
The story writes itself
into the fiction of history unless the homies still here don't allow it by
lending evidence to an eloquence of living on my part, pointing them
to my private papers, to the drafts that keep my promise evident to
the larger world because I ultimately couldn't without a physical form.

In the end, once they dig through my records and come up with
nothing but a few paid-off moving violations, they'll discover that
I didn't lack control in my life as they assumed; I lacked control *over*
my life. I could've had a JD and still lacked jurisdiction; somebody
close to me told me I had the juice and then I ended up getting juiced.

A tragedy. A regrettable mistake. A wake-up call.
In eternal sleep
I have the option of counting the bullets like sheep over and over or
counting the sheepish in all the sleepy towns so obviously I'll do both
and make my peace with the very state of emergency somehow being

less than urgent. Funny. My time here was too short but now I have all the time in the world to make my mark.

Mama, I'm going
to be a scar.

It's Important I Remember

THAT THERE'S A DIFFERENCE BETWEEN A HUMAN BEING AND A PERSON—

which comes to mind each time
I see them kiss a dog on the mouth.

A dog's mouth is cleaner than a human's

only because our best friends cannot say
the things acquaintances do about us.
Yesterday the choice word was *infestation*;
today it will be something else because it has to be
for things to carry on normatively.

That used to mean a house in the suburbs,
a trimmed lawn and picket fence, two children
and a hyperactive puppy to toss the Frisbee to;
that used to mean people tensed up when the
moving vans came barreling down the block. It still does.

But, anyway, I really do love myself a pooch,
have kept two such companions thus far in life.

The first of them slept in a cage at night;

the second only had to slip past an electric fence.

What I'm saying is that I've evolved on the issue of incarceration.

An animal with a given name isn't an animal anymore.

I recall his body lying in the street for hours,

like a dehydrated dog resting on its side,

panting. Except

there was no panting anymore, his lungs deflated like unused footballs.

My chest rises and falls faster the more I anger.

My blood carries narrative.

I hear whistles most days that it seems my neighbors can't.

My parents gave me a name out of love.

In the script of a film I love, a Sicilian crime boss selling narcotics

said that we're animals, that we deserve to lose our souls.

All it takes is a little provocation and the teeth are prone.

I'm talking about dogs here.

Nothing will love a man better or be more steadfast.

I love hard, but I need to love harder.

In Latin, *Homo sapiens* means *wise man*.

I am what I am, think and therefore.

I recognize the games being played on the big board:

putting people in cages, changing names to numeric codes.

People don't talk about that as much

as they talk about their pets, I find.

We give dogs the bones we'd prefer to be buried.

The first human remains were actually found in Africa,

dating back hundreds of thousands of years.

Just the other day, somebody told me to go back there

as if I could do so without taking them with me.

Into me. Into tenderness.

I wait by the door for them to return

before the streetlights flicker alive.

It's Important I Remember
THAT JESUS WEPT—

a few times on record but most famously
in the company of sad Mary and Martha

after Lazarus passed, shade cast over their
faces by the shadow of their brother's life.

Now, just so you know, Jesus of Nazareth
was capital G fo'real, almost to the level

of having his own face tatted on his back,
name below in Gothic lettering; he arranged

a life lesson out of a dear friend falling ill
to the point of death, planned to say to all

the gathered mourners by way of miracle:
Follow me, have faith that I can restore you

to good standing with the Almighty above us.
So he showed up to the somber function late

on purpose—real blickity-black behavior
in my Bible—to find Lazarus had dissolved

into memory, as he'd recognized would happen
without his hand involved, even from afar.

Both in knowing all and in having all power,
there was no logical reason for Jesus to weep

as he did here, but, having a human heart,
he was moved to tears by how torn up these

sisters were, synthesized and spread their
anguish throughout his own brown body.

It comforts me to know the divine can cry
for us, the Dirty Dirty's dirty. It was written

that he called to the body and in the calling
it became a house once again, the man who

I think of as Big Laz walking out the tomb
the way Crips walk into it, a walk that we've

imitated from California on one coast out to
the Carolinas on the other whether we tried

explicitly or not. This whole episode is why
we've rolled deep as river for the Son of Man,

why our aunties' aunties hang his picture on
their living room walls, his robing as white as

assumed innocence, Afro picked to perfection.
Since they speak as if we are the most sinful

people here, it must mean he bore that cross
for us disproportionately, the same cross we

dangle from our craned necks adorned in gold,
the beacon that leads us back from death after

death has taken us, as if the bullet was never
borne, body breathing in light like a church.

It's Important I Remember

THAT THEY DON'T HAVE THE TOOLS TO CRITIQUE ME—

what she told me. What I honor. *They*, as unambiguous as Lyrae is:
black, bard, badass; svelte with flourishing braids; a singularity and

somehow all of them gathered as one like tributaries to the mouth of
the river of God—Gwendolyn and Lucille and June and—and I can't

count all the ways I was saved that day, emerging wet from the ritual
to find myself sitting in some stranger's living room, a writer who'd

been pushed out of their homeland by its persecutions, pulled into
America on the promise of asylum, the same America that commits

my own kind to institutions with routine and rarely second thoughts
signaling the presence of conscience, and while we're on the subject

of right and wrong, know I'd read the news recently and retreated far
into my unfeeling before I received the blessing of her timely word,

walking in bloody boots through hallways leading to the chambers
where tenderness is said to rest in all of us by symbology, but then

I was called outside my bones again. And let me tell you, my friend:
You've never seen light before you've seen it. I swear, it's as if with

the snap of a finger I could recite the very definition of gold without
needing to run yolk from the promise of a child, a happy day's glow

spilling into the street like July's laughter from a fire hydrant as we
left the house with folk who loved words and loved us—loved *us*—

so expansively. And less than two nights later we're all throwing our
asses in a circle, cuttin' up, working up what was an effortless sweat,

undeterred even as the music skipped on every hiccup of the fraying
wires, tethered just as strenuously to joy as ever, like always, trying

to catch a good breath, but I paid it no mind, no mind, no mind—no,
I wasn't absent upstairs exactly, I was hyperpresent; what a ghost is

to death I was to life, inside everything simultaneously—the sub and
the synth, the blown-off roof and the hole-stomped floor, the rise of

their chests and the fall—and only *nigga* returned me to this plane:
my nigga, *my nigga*, a lyric left on my lower lip like the sweet after-

burn of Hennessy, but yo, it's like I was being called for, called out
of need since I know that word only has such resonance in a world

where we ain't free. And, nah, we ain't free, if you were wondering.
There are no shackles on me your eyes can see but none that I can't

feel as if they were appendages divided from me by the occurrence
of civil war, a set of chimeless chains that could be yanked on and

bring me, even at my most upright, to my knees. And if it happens—
again—I suppose I could pray, there, at my literally lowest moment,

immersed in the mess they've made that I'm tasked with cleaning
up for the commendation of pennies. I hope I don't get shot while

genuflect since that's apparently a thing now in this country, but I
worry such a selfish ask won't have sufficient fuel to reach heaven,

that the bastardized sparrow will burn up in the atmosphere as easily
as tissue paper. And I recognize I'm rambling now, but I'm likewise

increasing my odds of bumping into the point of all this since inside
the milk of me something was stirred by what she said, but it's hard

to translate a muscular language to a verbal one just as it's hard to
relate to folk who don't consider their own demise fifty 'leven times

a day at least, and for that relapse not to be an injurious ideation but
an itch of practicality. What I wouldn't pay for the chance to not pay

attention to every little thing—how they talk near me and how they
talk when they believe I'm nowhere near, what they do or don't do

with each other that they do or don't do with me, the questions they
feel quite content to ask me and the ones they never seem to though

I leave the door open, the window, the bleeding heart. I know them
so well, people who wouldn't know me from the next in the lineup;

I know them so intimately you'd think I love them all, and the gag is
that I do, by some undesired miracle, and that is part of all this, too.

To say they don't deserve my time is an obvious statement, but they
take it anyway because it's all they know, evident as I recount every

transgression taking seconds off my time on this earth, summing up
to years, almost to the point I'm gone already, in response to which

I either swallow spit or spit out ellipses. Ask the wounded wall what
I know of restraint, the manifesto I'd pen with what pours out from

my punctured knuckles, though perhaps the poet was signaling that,
all along, I've been teaching the most important life lesson merely by

domesticating rage, confining it inside the margins of the flesh that
my parents made for me, the page my life is written against each day

in corrective red ink. And this seems like the appropriate moment
to divulge that her sermon came during a dialogue about poetic craft

of all things, but if poetry can't be applied to how one moves through
this world then I see very little worth in it, which is where it started

for me. Poetry was a dead white thing in my life once, at the bottom
of the trash can with the doll of Jesus they'd tried pawning off on me

back in Catholic school, but luckily I already knew one for us, by us,
and thus found the inner strength to soldier through the barren winter

of lyrical delight rocking a pair of big-ass Timberlands and other on-
trend threads a person of greater gravitas could've filled out better

around the shoulders. But I digress—since what I really mean to be
speaking on is how the Cavalier poets weren't really doing it for me

during high school, not because their explicit sexuality or their taste
for material excess and ambitious proximity to the throne were such

disagreeable subjects to me, at the time revisiting rap's mafioso era,
but because when we painted those same pictures as we preferred to,

our tongues spiraling like ballerinas and bullets, they sought the ban
on sale or talked down on it as being absent of any artistic merit, as if

a nation's worth of people surviving subjugation is more science than
art anyway, for if that were true, then we wouldn't have a culture and

America wouldn't have great product to push to the rest of the planet
aside from all the bombs it seems much keener on dropping casually

like Funkmaster Flex, and I'd already grown tired in my young age,
so tired, of trying to prove I'm not stupid even above trying to prove

I'm smart. And those who doubt there's a difference have digging
to do, deep into their pockets to get me what I'm owed for damages,

for emotional distress and all things it's been made feasible to sue for
with solid legal representation. Funny, I once longed to be a lawyer,

little fool that I was, my back against a brick wall painted by spotlight,
rifles lined and aiming, in that night's vision—legal fluency seemed

the only option for release from this burden because it's the language
my nemeses speak in. I do know bad English from black, but I know

power even better because I've brushed up against it just as a person
in any number of neighborhoods around here may have brushed up

against a police officer. Maybe it's needless to say I didn't go down
an attorney path; I actually don't have a plan at all these days except

evading the bullet and also the bullet points corporations thrive on,
as if any of this is simple, as if I, symptom of systemic dysfunctions

enveloped by skeleton and skin, am something simple. I'd only ever
be two-dimensional if airbrushed on a blank T-shirt and even that

would show depth to someone's esteem for who I was with no one
else nearby, and all this means is that there is more to me or anyone

alike than being menace or miscreant, minstrel or misanthrope, or
murdered as all four would be with equal fanfare. But what I really

want is to know what they feel when their black friend dies in that
typical way, for it's maybe the only thing I don't know about them,

while we practice poker faces and draft FAQs. Forget seeing eye to
eye for a second. Set aside the particular grammars of forgiveness

we use without pulling up the problem's root: Do they still feel full
people if they put the hammer down? And when they can't answer,

make note that I can because I have those tools and also others that
shall remain nameless in order to remain purposeful. That's how I

prefer it, besting all desertions of their decency, which I say since
you've caught me rare and raw tonight, sipping off the bottle top,

slurring my songs, hitting my two-step on beat every. single. time.
Damn—how blessed they are to be able to watch me work around

them—as illegibly as what the miraculous Phillis Wheatley wrote
all over her master's walls, owned in the moment, I feel, solely by

an ambition toward self-definition I also try applying prodigiously,
bringing them to speechlessness, a shaming kind of silence saying

listen, leave me be because there's no explaining me, thus there's
no exploiting me: what only a history under thumb and foot helps

grasp before letting go, for one's own good even more than mine.

It's Important I Remember

THAT ALL I HAVE TO DO IS STAY BLACK AND DIE—

and nothing could come easier.

Even my mama beating the black off me
would only make me blacker: no diggity,

no doubt. And no doubt I've seen rough houses and rough-
housing in my day; *I'm no criminal, but I know criminals*

is common bio within our rectangular borders,
but they broke law that was already broken to begin with
so what does it even matter.

I admit we've got some kinks to comb out,
but we're no worse than anybody else is.

We're *for better or worse,*
through thick and thin about our own.

Black love is black magic is something you can't touch;
our natural air might as well be our natural hair.

We get as loud with light about each other
as the moon does on a country night,
talking like the queen's English with its pants sagging,
and I'm no exception to the stereo settings.

I say *I'm black and I'm proud* with my whole chest,
put an S on my pecs for my dearest peoples—
joy in a bold-typeface body language.

This is my house, my yard, my rules:
I ain't turning down the music for nobody.

Y'all been sleeping too cozy around here anyway.
Don't say we're disturbing the peace
when you can't even define what peace is:

Anything done at my expense
you're damn well going to pay me for.

As handsomely as I am.

~~09.17.1787~~

insure domestic tranquility

It's Important I Remember

THAT THE RIGHT TO KEEP AND BEAR ARMS IS THE SECOND AMENDMENT—

not the first.   The first enshrined freedom
of religion; freedom of speech; freedom of the press; freedom

to peaceably assemble; the right to petition the Government
for a redress of grievances.

Ergo, in theory, the firearm comes behind the reason to use it,
                        being necessary to security of a free

State.   *Security* is the justification some, State
        or citizen, provide when there is no longer another person

alive to argue otherwise—therefore, the firearm comes before a sound
reason to use it, which is unconstitutional in a spiritual sense.

It doesn't take a judge or jury to resolve all this;
                                it takes a just god.

Just God is all some of us say we have left to believe in,
and even that's slipping

                            with each silver bullet sliding into chamber
that refuses to retire there, that gets paid leave after it leaves

the barrel and leaves a wake in its wake. Grief—
a word of the same linguistic root as
                                        grievance, unredressed.

In red: the petals of flowers, a husk undressed
of all pronouns save for *it*.

It's Important I Remember

THAT THE ONLY THING WE HAVE TO FEAR IS FEAR ITSELF—

for it immobilizes far less frequently than it thrusts us forward.

Fear funds the police department and the FBI.
Fear designed the suburb and the housing project in opposition.

Fear is building the wall right now how it built the schoolhouse,
how it built the prison and made those two synonyms by sight.

When you look into my eyes you see fear
because *you* are afraid of *me*:

Fear is your reflection, reveals you to you
by way of my form, and always you turn away, turn away, turn away.

I'm not afraid: I'm full of your fear.

It spills out of me like water but is indeed a thing thicker than that—
onto the floor, into the street.

Thoroughly sinister or evil.

Indicative of condemnation or discredit.

Characterized by hostility or angry discontent.

So reads *black* by Noah Webster's hand, a man who is no poet.

Only you could write us into these words— your fear

spills from books, like ink; from newspapers and magazines, like ink;
from penal codes, like ink—embraces permanence, permeates,

portends the dispatch from the nearest precinct into my ordinary life
on an ordinary night, the road sorrowed slick by sideways rain.

When that particular President Roosevelt addressed fear,
my people were not his primary concern:

Tens of millions of white folk had been reduced to a diet of dust,
as many always have been, and as many, I worry, always will be.

It's been the same deal with them since forever. They'll be fed
hope or they'll be fed lies, and I can always tell what they've ingested:

every time we encounter at the eyes, if I see the flame flicker, faintly;
if darkness floods the smallness of the space they are, it will spill over.

Whether the man that is a mirror is shattered in that moment, who knows—
but one can pray not because one can still fear God.

It's Important I Remember

THAT IT COSTS EXTRA TO ADD CHEESE ON A WHOPPER—

I hear the late Big L's voice in my head whenever I think about it,
gloating that he wouldn't give a woman ten cents to get the cheese.

Misogynist though the source may be, it did teach me a sly lesson
about consideration, that the smallness of a gesture does not speak

to its level of significance. They said, when asked, that they offered
him the burger as a form of sustenance after he'd not eaten for days,

but I wonder whether they gave him the additional delight, if they
considered him in that intimate way, allowed him to cut to the front

of the line of their concerns, called him *Dylann* rather than *Roof*.

I've been to Burger King enough to know the Whopper is the first item
on the menu: a flame-grilled, four-ounce beef patty, lettuce, tomatoes, onions,

pickles, mayo, and ketchup on a sesame seed bun. They would've confronted
the choice almost immediately: whether or not to bestow an act of kindness

on top of an act of kindness upon a young man who murdered nine people
at Bible study before their creator and his. I want to say they wouldn't

opt for the American cheese the way my mom or dad used to for me,
taking charge over my pleasure, perhaps rewarding me; but, then again,

the officer was already waiting in line that day, maybe even aligned—
like the beliefs of parents and children tend to be—considering all I know

about policing in this country that a delectable yellow slice is named for.
That I paid extra for. That made me weep, being as familiar as it was.

I guess, in the end, it is the little things that matter: that gratify, that hurt.

It's Important I Remember

THAT THE FEELING OF AN EYE ON ME BURNS—

just recall, that is, how the human eye works: Light strikes
the retina as it does somber flooring through the window;
the photoreceptors transform the light into electrical signals
sent through optic nerves to the brain, which interprets
and projects the picture in all its vibrancy and detail.

Recall that electricity creates heat when the flow of electrons
is resisted, when the conductor is overwhelmed, and the energy
is converted into the natural antidote for frigidity.

When you look at me with unbridled affection,
there is a genuine warmth in your eyes:
electricity.
When you look at me with rage or anger,
there is wildfire in you, a calamitous conflagration.

Most about me that overwhelms strangers' circuitry
is completely imagined:

My frame is stretched five feet toward the sky like
a bear and fills out with muscle;
my IQ bottoms out
below the average goldfish;
a hippopotamus
assumes my hippocampus and I recover
how to make violence out of peace.

I can tease out when someone is trying to retrofit
me into that nastiest of English words, the one
that ended up in our mouths as a reclamation—

their eyes putting small burns on my back
like the tip of a lit cigarette against a forearm.

There have been instances of this in my life,
but one in particular continues to hassle me.

There was no police officer nearby, no ominous pickup
truck with a Confederate flag decal, nothing like that—

it was just me, in a bookstore

with a single shopkeeper

behind a tiny desk, a woman

who was the color words

most often are printed on,

while I'm the typical tint

of what is pressed

to the page.

And I was being pressed, silently; I was being
followed as I combed the shelves, checking spines
against the titles on my syllabus, a first-year
freshly on campus. There hadn't been any offer
of assistance. I know I felt a need to do the opposite
of take my time, as my body boiled beneath my
brand-new school sweatshirt, as smoke began to fill
the aisles formed from stacking books to the ceiling.

There was nothing dangerous about this situation,
yet it sticks with me all these years later, though,
I recall, they never wanted us to read to begin with,
to learn how the eye works, to be able to articulate
the function of surveillance: burning us all alive
from the inside out.

It's Important I Remember

THAT THE ROOT OF THE PROBLEM IS THE ROOT—

my vigilance (from French *vigilance*)	and	your vigilantism (from Spanish *vigilante*)
my vigilance (from Latin *vigilantia*)	and	**your** vigilantism (from Latin *vigilantem*)
my **vigilance** ("wakefulness") ("watchfulness") ("attention")	and	your vigilantism ("watchful") ("anxious") ("careful")
my vigilance	and (from Latin *vigil*)	your **vigilantism**
my vigilance	and ("watchful") ("awake")	your vigilantism
my vigilance (*woke*)	and	**your vigilantism** (*choke*)
my vigil (*sleep*)	and	**your vigil** (*sheep*)

It's Important I Remember

THAT GEORGE ZIMMERMAN ISN'T WHITE—

the one sad drip from his daddy that made him wholly
insufficient when scrutinized against the knot of bloodlines

his Peruvian mother embodied. This is conceivably where his
woman troubles began, with a sentiment that his mother

took something from him by virtue of being who she was.
Thus, he marks himself Hispanic on his voter registration form,

though in Florida the term links through exiles to a right-wing
angle on law and order, an adjacency putting him closer

to the truth in his heart that, indeed, he is a white man
with white powers: *underage drinking* and *domestic violence*

and *criminal mischief* and *second-degree murder* and free to
do them all again, if only he hadn't auctioned off the gun,

what a real white man wouldn't do due to its pricelessness—
first for besting the boy's body, then for making the man famous.

It's Important I Remember

THAT WHITENESS IS ONLY AN ORIENTATION—

a matter of relation and position.
One less-textbook theory of relativity reads

that anyone can choose their family
outside the bond of blood.

I have friends turned relatives
who never let me forget

that cane sugar best sweetens the iced tea
or that cow's milk is kind to the bones;

how beautiful an ivory dress is
on love standing in mirror to love.

Normatively, human beings see color
in everything, and it's allowable

to admit that aloud. Even as I consider this,
snow falls without any sense of speed

and blankets the ground
gorgeously blank:

It's not this sight that I can't stand
but the freezing cold that comes with it—

my displeasure isn't for what I look
upon with my own eyes

but for the feeling of discomfort
that it brings down on me

with a chilling intention.

~~11.08.2016~~

inevitability

It's Important I Remember

THAT LYNDON B. JOHNSON SAID, "WE HAVE LOST THE SOUTH FOR A GENERATION"—

supposedly to an aide upon signing the Civil Rights Act
of 1964. The fact of this hasn't been firmly established,

but the truth has. My own mother was barely four months old
at the time; my father was elsewhere in the big-shouldered city,

not yet four years, writing on walls, perhaps, like an announcement
of inevitability, his growth into softer powers inspiring a backlash

as prophesized by the president. Theirs was to be the generation of us
who watched losses pile where our people left from most recently like

birds with busted compasses under their breasts, and, yes, their eyes did
witness large swaths of land in this country turn redder and redder like

white men's anger read on their cheeks: Mississippi deep in blood like
Alabama deep in blood like Louisiana deep in blood and so forth across

the old Confederacy, still alive, still breathing. I've now made three
decades myself, a boy born as my parents neared that trinity of tens,

now a poet watching vote returns, working through predictive math,
waiting for the damn volta, for the moment these tired, these poor

huddled masses wake up to their own exploitation and set aside
color enough to squad up. But some predictions are built to last,

at least until the last Ku Klux Klansman dies childless, as lonely as
a Stonewall Jackson statue toppled over like a small-town drunk and

even then, not even, I'm afraid. Someone inside me says that they want to
go home and someone else inside me says that they can never return there.

It's virtually impossible to have a good sense of direction in this country, or
to find a moral in its history, not while I still see so much blood, brilliant and

menacing, spilled across the Bible Belt, that fails to redeem any of us, though
if it's pointed out, they'll say that's not blood at all. *No, that's just democracy*

at work—and maybe it is,
I'm afraid. Maybe it is.

It's Important I Remember

THAT POLITICS IS A CONTACT SPORT—

as evidenced by the paraphernalia in his locker,
a token of patronage for the president of the United States,
a man he and his team's owner are known to be partial to.

It sits there in full view of the television cameras, almost
pornographic, explicitly red, tattooed with a tagline in white
lettering that makes some shiver and others frenzy.

> Fanatic: The label *fan* shortens this word
> or shortens a fuse, most certainly.

He, the president, said *get that son of a bitch*
off the field and people exploded into exclamation points
while an ancestor took a knee in me: anthem, anathema.

Back when, the outrage dissipated so quickly
over their deflating of the football, caught red-handed
from applying pressure, but the outrage over deflating
the black person's lungs elapsed even faster, their killer
caught red-handed from blood, the phrase's Scottish origin.

How funny, then, for all these famous men involved
in deadly games to get off scot-free, without a substantial tax;
how much it hurts, then, that they get to skate and play the hero.

Sadly, we're here yet again: the star of star quarterbacks
flashing his endorsement smile, teeth purely white, after
his latest Super Bowl victory. The commentators sing
his praises, call him undoubtedly the greatest of all time,
the iconic leader of the Patriots, never to be forgotten.

I reflect a moment and recall the original patriot
was a black man shot dead by the British in Boston;
I reflect a moment and can't recall his name
because there have been too many shot dead like him since.

At times, I'm heartened hardly anybody outside this country
cares about our gridiron game; always I'm disheartened
less than nobody inside this country cares about us,
even though we're sacrificing on that field, taking shots.

To the torso.   To the head.
For less than millions.   For less than nothing.

It's Important I Remember

THAT PEOPLE VOTED FOR DONALD TRUMP BECAUSE OF ECONOMIC ANXIETY—

so it's been said, but that's a slick little lie, even if it was considered "credible" reporting at the time. Imagine paying all those tens of thousands of dollars for a bachelor's degree, for a master's degree in journalism, and not being required to take a single African American studies course. Imagine being a journalist with influence and reach who is unable or, worse yet, unwilling to tell the truth in active voice.

As the saying goes: *It could not be me*.

My decision about what college to attend was a compromise of impulses. My most important criteria were: not too close to home (so that I'd grow and have more independence); located in or in immediate proximity of a large city (where there'd be black people who existed who were not me); top-notch academics (as I desired a cerebral challenge and I'm a competitive person beneath my easygoing demeanor); prestige (translation: respect). My father didn't really care what I did, but not in that lazy way we expect of many dads—he simply trusted I was already thinking sharply, as he felt I'd always done. My mother, though, stood on pragmatism: *Make sure you can go out there and get a job when you graduate. You need to be able to provide for yourself.*

She had a point, one that would be repeated hundreds of thousands of times by the time I graduated with lethal amounts of red in the ledger, though I understood it even as a high school senior, and years before that, in fact. I was always a practical kid; I'm a practical adult now, and I hate that about me. Being practical is a way to survive, but it's no way to live.

In the end, I enrolled at the Wharton School of the University of Pennsylvania, where Donald Trump and Elon Musk once matriculated, where so many big-time investment bankers earned their pedigree, the very ones who tanked the economy back in 2008 before I even stepped foot in one of those classrooms. I don't regret my decision, really; I'm still here, after all. I have a job that provides for a comparatively comfortable life. A lot of folks like me can't say that. A lot of folks like me can't say anything anymore.

A list of people to hold the most powerful job in the world, as of April 2008:

1. George Washington (white guy, slave owner)
2. John Adams (white guy)
3. Thomas Jefferson (white guy, slave owner, black baby mama)
4. James Madison (white guy, slave owner)
5. James Monroe (white guy, slave owner, Liberia dude)
6. John Quincy Adams (white guy, his daddy's son)
7. Andrew Jackson (white guy, slave owner, slave trader, Trail of Tears)
8. Martin Van Buren (white guy, slave owner)
9. William Henry Harrison (white guy, slave owner)
10. John Tyler (white guy, slave owner)
11. James K. Polk (white guy, slave owner)
12. Zachary Taylor (white guy, slave owner)
13. Millard Fillmore (white guy)
14. Franklin Pierce (white guy)
15. James Buchanan (white guy)
16. Abraham Lincoln (white guy, Illinois, Civil War, emancipation, shot)
17. Andrew Johnson (white guy, slave owner)
18. Ulysses S. Grant (white guy, slave owner by technicality, Union general)
19. Rutherford B. Hayes (white guy)
20. James A. Garfield (white guy, shot)
21. Chester A. Arthur (white guy)
22. Grover Cleveland (white guy)
23. Benjamin Harrison (white guy)
24. Grover Cleveland (wait, again?)
25. William McKinley (white guy, shot)
26. Theodore Roosevelt (white guy)
27. William Howard Taft (white guy)
28. Woodrow Wilson (white guy, World War I, super-duper racist)
29. Warren G. Harding (white guy)
30. Calvin Coolidge (white guy)
31. Herbert Hoover (white guy)
32. Franklin D. Roosevelt (white guy, Great Depression, New Deal, World War II, Japanese internment)
33. Harry S. Truman (white guy, atomic bombs)

34. Dwight D. Eisenhower (white guy)
35. John F. Kennedy (Irish Catholic white guy, shot)
36. Lyndon B. Johnson (white guy, civil rights, Great Society, Vietnam)
37. Richard Nixon (white guy, crook)
38. Gerald Ford (white guy)
39. Jimmy Carter (white guy, nice guy)
40. Ronald Reagan (white guy . . .)
41. George H. W. Bush (white guy)
42. Bill Clinton (white guy, "first black president")
43. George W. Bush (white guy, his daddy's son, war on terror)
44. . . .
45. . . .
46. . . .
47. . . .

The same question, every single year:
What do you want to be when you grow up?

That's such a Caucasian-ass question
if we're being honest.

I just wanted to grow up.
All I wanted

was to grow up.

In business school, I moved away from more quantitative subjects, such as finance and accounting, toward disciplines like management and marketing. It wasn't a loathing of math that steered me in this direction but, instead, an appreciation for arenas where names have the chance of being as important as numbers. This had always been true for me.

Kindergarten through twelfth grade, my favorite subject in school was history: I loved ancient history, loved European history, loved world history. Above all else, though, I loved American history—how it read like a fairy tale, how I'd snicker to myself at just about everything the teacher would say. Luckily for me, I grew up knowing a whole host of historians, enough to catch the zingers that flew over my classmates' heads (first Thanksgiving, anyone?), though they weren't recognized as jokes by any accredited institution. The historians I called on had no doctorates. They had no master's degrees. Some had no college education at all, and others had never even finished high school. But their eyes had seen it all. Their eyes had seen all they could handle. My parents, my grandparents—they never wanted that for me. They wanted me to be secure.

The day after Trayvon Martin went out for Skittles and the day after Michael Brown was left lying in the street for hours and the day after Tamir Rice held a toy gun for the last time and the day after Walter Scott was face down in the dirt and the day after Sandra Bland got pulled over and the day after Clementa Pinckney oversaw his last Bible study and the day after Eric Garner's daughter was crying on the news and the day after Jordan Davis didn't turn down the music fast enough and the day after Michelle Cusseaux had her wellness check and the day after Korryn Gaines last saw her child and the day after Freddie Gray was snapped in half and the day after they lit up Laquan McDonald like those golden arches and the day after Philando Castile served students lunch for the last time, I went to work.

And the day after.

And the day after.

And the day after.

And because I did, I got paid.

I was secure—

at least some might say.

The day after Donald Trump was elected president of the United States, I went to work as if nothing had happened. And it hadn't, at least in the sense that what occurred wasn't out of the ordinary or outside the realm of possibility, but perspective is a funny thing. A lot of folks around the office were visibly concerned, hanging their heads solemnly, talking with a decided lack of energy in sharp contrast to what they'd demonstrated less than twenty-four hours before when so many felt they would be voting for the first woman to ever hold the presidency in this nation's history. I hear side conversations analyzing what went wrong, everything from African American voters not turning out in high enough numbers to James Comey's memo to deeply rooted sexism and misogyny, but none of this is indicative of something going wrong. No, this is how things work around here, around America, all areas thereof. Where have these people been? Why are they crying today if I never have? What do they have to lose except something I could never attain to begin with?

I have a vivid childhood memory of when I learned a cousin of mine had been murdered. It was the eve of the school year, and my mother was dropping me off at her mother's house before she headed to work. The room was dim with only a single strand of light slipping through the gap between the curtains like the one between my top front teeth when smiling, the only source of warmth in the space. My granny was sitting down in that green upholstered chair pressed up against the wall on what was my left side, my mom standing just beyond the doorway, and me, floating in the vicinity like a thought bubble left unfilled. There was nothing to be said, but there were things to be done by each of us. And we did them. Even as a child, I had a job to do. Rain or shine or rain or rain or rain.

“Also among the slightly odd findings of the poll, 18% of respondents who felt that Mr. Trump was not qualified to be president nonetheless voted for him, as did 20% of those who felt he did not have the necessary temperament.”

—*BBC News, on a poll from Edison Research*

From the very beginning,
what they always expressed

to my parents

was how nice and
well mannered I am.

Teachers.
Neighbors.

Complete strangers.

I always took it as a compliment.

I took it the wrong way.

~~01.05.2021~~

sick and tired of
being sick and tired

It's Important I Remember

THAT THERE'S A MARCH TOMORROW—

but I've already passed the memo to the intended recipient.

I'd learned my place years ago, the first and final time I was carried
through the streets of New York City by a current of womanhood,
when I received an invitation that I should have respectfully declined
in recognition and consideration.
                                        Tomorrow isn't about me. Rightfully,
it's about all the she out there, my wife one among many women with woe.

The man has made it clear it's his world now, every pearl in every oyster;
we'd let the unconsented grabbing go too easily and now his hands
will be on everything, the Supreme Court and Congress in the bag
like red baseball caps, bronzer, and too many small campaign donations.

Wifey says she doesn't trust it, what happened today and what will happen
tomorrow.
                    Not every woman is born with pearls to clutch within reach;
not every woman needs to buy a pearl of wisdom from the bestsellers list.

My wife enjoys a good oyster, loves few things more than a dollar delicacy
during happy hour.
                                                            These are unhappy times.
Our country is hurrying toward danger,
so women are hurrying to DC in a demonstration of intent, if not of power.

Where were they all before, she doesn't ask me so much as agitate the silences
in the developing news story. I'd learned my place years ago, placing my
hand against her back whenever she'd come home with a story all her own
about some lady at the office who seemed intimidated or unsettled by her,
who offered unsolicited advice to "be more approachable."
                                                                        I've seen the moon
fall across her face in those moments. I bring bottles of red wine to the problem,
perhaps a box of Peeps, not to solve anything but to boost her spirits. Yet tonight,
for some reason, I opted, instead, for a lollipop that matches her deepest lipstick.

Tomorrow, in another black woman's mouth, she will see the lollipop again
on TV, all over social media, despite trying to duck the crowd. Her odds
of failing to? Based on exit polling, chances were about 53 percent;

the sign that other black woman holds in the picture—while surrounded by
women in pussy hats—reads *Don't forget: White women voted for Trump.*

Two suckers dissolve into a rush of cherry while a larger crowd cheers.

It's Important I Remember

THAT SOJOURNER TRUTH HADN'T SUFFERED ENOUGH—

apparently being born the lowest class
of noun wasn't adequately tragic.

Steering one's life story over the hills of low Dutch
and English was too elevated an exercise for an illiterate.

Her Northern narrative of enslavement could
weaken the moral authority of the abolitionist cause,
so it needed to be revised southward
with diction and cadence.

Birthing five babies, one of whom
was of her legal captor rather than her beloved,
was eight labors too few to evoke sufficient sympathy.

The hard labor: perfect.
The beatings: even better for being even worse.

Four bills of sale on her back were forced moves
that could help propel two movements forward.

She could escape the institution of inherited servitude;

she could best a white man in court to reclaim her stolen son;

she could find strength through Jesus Christ
and toll the church bell at the back of her throat;

she could name herself anew and travel the country preaching—
but couldn't be allowed an authentic portrait in print.

Ain't I a woman?   is a question Truth never asked and never would.
I am a woman's rights   is right factually; is right spiritually;

is a statement with a single interpretation that left no room
for Frances Dana Barker Gage's editorial intent

to wash for whiteness—with the blackness of ink—
Sojourner's unshakeable voice:
the substance being sold to support the shadow.

It's Important I Remember

THAT FANNIE LOU HAMER KEPT THE PHONE OFF THE HOOK—

because she'd already answered the calling, she knew
what threats were on the other line.

There was no need to add ringing to that already in her ears:
the bangs of sixteen errant bullets bouncing against her eardrums;
the drumming of the police officer's blackjack,
held in one black inmate's hand and then another's,
against her exposed body at the Law's order.

What didn't kill her
                                        didn't kill her,

so she wheeled on toward freedom—with the Freedom Ballot,
Freedom Summer—singing hymns to her comrades the whole bus ride.

By the time they arrived in Atlantic City for the DNC,
the convention hall was buzzing. There was a pulse
that defied death as she did any other day. Fannie Lou
came to represent, to inoculate a Mississippi strain
of illiberalism within the democracy, to take a literal seat
at the proverbial table that she and her people deserved.

This assertion of principle presented an urgent political problem,
as even the president of the United States tried to black out
the black woman whose hands were no strangers
to the soil of the situation, being on the ground, in the dirt,
from sharecropping in the cotton fields to planting
the seeds of resistance in the hearts of students.

The news cameras cut away to the White House
as she spoke before the credentials committee that afternoon,
but she was so compelling they cut back to her testimony that night.

In questioning America, in undermining its very sense of soul,
Hamer hit the nail on the head for a lot of working men and women

watching in their living rooms, the nail that closed the coffin
on President Johnson's chances of carrying Mississippi
against Barry Goldwater come November, the beginning
of a fall of one sort but, also, the rise of something truer,

and somewhere over the Delta, God thundered.

It's Important I Remember

THAT SOUTH CAROLINA SECEDED FIRST—

and, again, my country is at a crossroads.

This time, the guns are stowed away. The shots are
taken in the press and town halls filled with likely voters.

I'm watching the news segment with my granny
in her kitchen on a Sunday after church service;

I distill what is being discussed on TV down to one question
and one answer, which is why I recall it with such ease,
even after all that's happened since,
or maybe because of it.

Three primary contests have already been called:
the caucuses in Iowa breaking for Barack Obama,
New Hampshire and Nevada boosting Hillary Clinton.

South Carolina shifts the map to the South, the next state
where ballots will be cast with a third of them
in the hands of black women.

Hillary has a modicum of cookout cache running back
to the popular presidency of her husband, Bill.

The Obamas, conversely, have hosted *and* been invited
to the cookout at different times,
and this is a determinative difference.

Billed as possible first vs. possible first,
the campaigns duke it out for votes
from the people with the most prominent duality in the state.

When President Clinton notes that Jesse Jackson won
the South Carolina primary in his unsuccessful bids
for the White House, he reveals that he isn't black after all.

Reverend Jesse Jackson lives within minutes of where we sit
in Chicago viewing South Carolinians opine on the race.

Jesse has come through our church many times;
the black church is full of women like a polling location.

If you believe identity is destiny, then the question
is rather obvious even if not explicitly stated:
What piece of themselves will black women select on Tuesday?

I won't be eligible to vote in Illinois until after it's too late,
but Granny has her answer, and she will become mine
to this and several questions hereafter.

Hers has nothing to do with the fact that Obama
is our home senator and everything to do
with the fact that Obama is our home senator.

What she says about it is folksy, and I can't do it justice here;
instead, I will translate as best as I can reminisce it:
You choose the thing you'll always be
over the thing they've always denied you are.

We already know who won—
or what side won, if you prefer.

It's Important I Remember

THAT ROSA PARKS WAS THE PERFECT CANDIDATE—

and I believe it's evident even in, perhaps, her most iconic photograph, the boycott's visual epilogue wherein Rosa rests with poise on the bus seat with a white male reporter behind her, her head turned to profile position, pupils focused through eyeglasses and window as if studying the future, her hands patiently placed in her lap atop a patterned dress. This image was carved from light months before she and her husband would leave the continued threats and harassments and head north, landing finally in Detroit, where they fell asleep to the sound of rumbling motors. She ended her story quietly, not as hectic as the early chapters when a woman of conventional refinements refused meekness and movement while, as she later recounted, darling Emmett's murder the next state over weighed down her wings. A married woman. Churchgoing woman. Involved-and-connected woman who jotted the deviled details in the office and out in the field after women like her had been violated, violently, by white men. Rosa was the one with no dirt under her fingernails. Rosa was the one with a coat of polish. Rosa was the one they could hold up stapled to a piece of lumber or print in all the papers, a seamstress so seamless a fit she'd decline to speak when asked to address the crowd. To finish her diploma twenty-odd years before, she had to learn that one divided by one is, indeed, one. To finish my diploma fifty-odd years after her famous arrest, I had to learn that Rosa Parks was both the problem and its solution. The math carries over time: that Montgomery bus lines were on the brink of bankruptcy after a full year of boycotting broke in the same direction the law did once the Supreme Court decided. The case didn't bear her name, but it wore her face, as did the Forever postage stamp that followed decades later: *the one*.

And when Mrs. Parks passed away in 2005, my classmate's father, Mr. Louis Freeman, the first African American chief pilot at Southwest Airlines—or any major US carrier—flew her body from Detroit to Montgomery for ceremonies, then to Baltimore and DC, and then, finally, back to Detroit. This might've given me a sense of closeness to her, emotionally, had I not already known her through the spirits of every single black person that her own personhood came to envelop like the mother we titled her as in praise of her immeasurable contributions to our forward movement in America; Rosa never bore one baby all her own, yet she was survived by her kids all the same.

It's Important I Remember

THAT ELLA BAKER WAS MARRIED TO THE MOVEMENT—

a man only once, her college sweetheart
from Shaw, but she set him free, so to speak,
just before she slipped south to Atlanta
to start working with the SCLC.

When she arrived at headquarters,
there was no headquarters—
unless one considered it the telephone booth
eating her few precious coins.

Eventually, a minister helped secure
office space that she furnished
and stocked with essential supplies,
making a home, which

wasn't what she signed up for since
Rustin and Stanley Levison were the ones who
put her name down for the gig, convincing Dr. King

that the woman Ella Baker was—
brilliant, educated, experienced in organizing—
was the man for the job.

Secretary of a certain nature, she was a notetaker
in the field, cultivating the grassroots
and keeping faith with the disaffected.

Baker was not someone who believed in kings
so there were frictions of philosophy
that tested her patience and kept her out

of Martin's inner circle, though she made sure
they could hear her from the next room over.

Strong people don't need strong leaders,
she believed devoutly, and none are stronger
than those who have survived

with marginal attention, in mind
paid to them and in material needs met,
so she left the position to be among them,
not intending to become a leader but to lead
people to themselves.

~~06.13.2020~~

my sister's keeper

It's Important I Remember

THAT HALLE BERRY IS THE ONLY BLACK WOMAN TO WIN AN ACADEMY AWARD FOR BEST ACTRESS—

as of this writing, though things can surely change, and may have changed
in the time between drafting and our minds meeting here on this very page,
though it's not unsurprising for things to remain static in a grander scheme,

gesturing toward our social structures, and if anything has changed since print,
or if the measure of difference is only a few degrees removed from a decade
her people couldn't vote in peacefully—unlike those who elected to honor her

on that noteworthy night—then Halle Berry remains a figure worth revisiting
every now and then, and though in this case I don't mean for *figure* to refer to
her physical composition, I also recognize the crux of this reflection rests upon

a distinctly visual allure, that the famous scene, should you be familiar with it,
has now crawled from a place of primal hunger onto the screens of your eyes,
that it has been made a moving picture again, given color and Dolby sound—

and when Halle is onstage to accept her award for a job well done, as she's
crying rivers that only her darkest foremothers have crossed at risk, nobody
can take their focus away from her nakedness, including me, even as I witness

her before us all, trying to clothe the shame of her being put in that position by
praising all the overlooked black starlets who came before her, and while I do
mean *shame* to reference the fact Berry is the first and, as of this writing, only

black woman to secure that most coveted trophy, I presume that you presumed
I was referring to the depiction of intimate acts that aroused the deep cynicism
in some of us regarding her selection or, worse, the sexism in us, the racism in

us, and that, I think, is a significant reason why things, while certainly able to,
never seem to change, not much and never soon enough. That's what the film
was about in one sense: Events will be allowed to proceed until the point there

are only two of us and no one more. I'll confess that I'm a man bettered only by the part of me you are, twisting movie lines into the context of our specific solitude, and I feel you'd then revise my attempt at poetry: *Y'all come from us,*

not the other way around, stepping off the porch and toward the blazing horizon as the curtain falls upon what we used to call a home, a country; as my blackness fades into yours with an emptied world awaiting a decision, finally yours alone

and, also, final.

It's Important I Remember

THAT FREDERICK DOUGLASS LEARNED HOW TO READ—

and Anna Murray Douglass, his first missus, did not.

Before her husband left boyhood's single digits,
his lessons in letters were swiftly ended by his new master—
intervening in his own wife's illegality—with the recognition
an ability to read ruins a slave's fit for enslavement.

As legend goes, this launched Frederick's pursuit of literacy
and the liberation it would deliver, but this poem, for one thing,
for once, is not about him in the first, though it must turn around
his decisions as Anna did whenever he disappeared, literally,
into his work, a literary man and lecturer in demand
running across borders like a sentence let off its chain.

Whereas her husband had come to be seen
as unfit for anything less than acclaim, Anna was seen
as unfit for him by many in the academy of abolitionists,
a woman so dark the marks of beauty couldn't be seen under sunlight,
a woman so dull in intellect she couldn't thumb
the autobiographies she was written out of.
The woman
who housed them in their organizing visits. The woman
who fed them with food from the soul. The woman
who tended to the tender-headed babies
and made the household math work;
the one who was no fugitive
herself but transformed her betrothed into one with her own coin and
connections, who harbored those to follow his footsteps to freedom.

What the renowned Frederick would want in a wife like Anna
wasn't mystery; she could skim the slants of people's bodies away
from hers—an alphabet of small indignities and silent sufferings—
who filed in and filled her bedrooms from wall to wall, even as
her spouse took flight to Seneca Falls to uplift women's suffrage.
What he wanted, what he needed, she provided despite the feeling of it.

Living in a marriage with a man wed to literatures and ideals
is something my own wife could tell you about. Of all the things
she will claim I've taught her over the years, how to read a poem
wouldn't be among them. I'm just like Mr. Douglass in a sense,
and less flattered by that than it sounds in verse, but maybe more than
Anna was by a missive in the mail accompanied by a husbandly sum
that might not have mentioned her name at all.

It's Important I Remember

THAT EVEN BEYONCÉ GOT CHEATED ON—

a woman who has everything, thus having everything
to lose, so much she couldn't stomach walking away from.

But I know there's a room, somewhere, that's been so
meticulously disheveled: shards of clarity splintered
across a hardwood floor, hangers stripped to collarbone,
an open window letting the secret out from the second story
with articles of clothing making for incomplete sentences.

Sobering surprise.
Stupefaction.

I think I love my wife.
I think,
I love my wife.

She raises her little fist to my face—and we wind up in riot,
laughing at this playful refrain in all our years of togetherness.

Let me clue you in on something: A threat isn't a promise
made in platinum or rose gold.
Feelings are like bone
in my finger or yours, the part of a living thing that lasts
after the living is finished.
She *loves* me
but says
the first time would be the last time, shaking her head
to shake off doubts of her conviction, not even a blink
the way light glints on the surface of a kitchen knife.

Blues in her left eye, funk in her right.

Now the little blue bird is chirping in the window again
with juicy celebrity gossip, and we go to bed wondering

aloud how lengthy Nia Long's night has been, but I have
a different woman to fear
                                                            slipping out of my own hands,
embroidered with nervous perspiration, and though I'm not
a selfish man compared to selfish men, there's the part of me—

there's the part of me that hurts for hurting her or her or
especially her that's right here with me: the risk she runs
that's trying to play safe.
                                                            Play safe as in *enact safety*;
    play safe as in *be safety*.

No man is so romantic that it prevents him from
stealing privileges off the back of one woman or every.

                                                    One woman married a poet.
                                                    One woman married a rapper.
It can be argued they are one
and the same.

I rode the elevator with her and her sister and a little girl
clutching the second's pinky for dear life, all that she can reach.

That's the last thing I remember
except for all the things I want to forget.

                                        The way a woman loves incriminates you—

how easily a vow is broken,
easier than a law
with no eyes on it;

how easily a vow is broken off,
easier than a law
with too many eyes on it.

                                                                        How badly I want

to be good to her, and how bad I am I don't get to decide,
but every day I'm not abandoned her assessment is clear:
not quite bad enough to drop a platinum album on my head,

or a *New York Times* Best Seller,
or even a single blade of paper

that, in my lifetime, I've seen
partition the highest of thrones,

the one the sun, once, never set on.

It's Important I Remember

THAT I BELIEVED I COULD FLY—

like the boys who got their sneakers
tangled in the telephone wires did,

running through that open door
framed by golden rays of light.

On a good day the sky above is blue
as blood appears to be flowing inside us

and I coveted that very symmetry,
the sensation of me in a sea of me.

That, it turns out, is an ask for godliness
as much as comfort, but I was only a boy

who cracked the shell of a woman
on his way into the world, wingless,

thus I was too immature to comprehend
the implications of calling on the clouds

for a favor, that it costs you in return.
What I could do, however, was watch

birds, study grace. When I was young,
there was a little girl in a movie I loved

who prayed for God to make her a bird
so she could fly far, far away, away from

her father's hands; I had no such delusion,
however cute it was to consider writing

against the cerulean page with the quills
on my arms. Somehow I knew, even then,

that to escape wasn't necessarily to be free—
so when I heard the song as the film opened,

I wasn't taken above but taken within,
where there is, like the sky, so much

blue and a boy like the boy I was to the world
dribbling a ball as bright as the setting sun.

I had an idol and an idle mind so the picture
projects as predictable to me now: I wanted

to pose midflight, to pirouette past defenders
on the court, have people applaud and toss

flowers at my flawless kicks. My hero—
the athlete, not the singer, though I did sing

that song with a special flame in my stomach,
stirred by it like all the rest. I heard his croon

in my head as much as on the airwaves,
while I tried to practice my free throws

in the school gym or my neighbor's driveway,
whenever I leapt toward the rim with the ball

rolling off my fingers and came back down
because, though angelic, I was still alive:

still here to have a dream even if not
to ever live it out, to pretend professions

with my friends and dart my eyes away from
that pretty girl when she looked at me since

it tickled a spot I couldn't name. I'll call her
Lola because it was the greatest compliment

in first grade. I just wanted to make the
league then; I forget what her wish was:

I want to say it was her sincere desire to
be a singer—just as common a dream

as mine, in that city and at that time, when
those men loomed above us, almost gods.

Michael, at least, was a true angel's name;
Robert, now, names something else entirely.

And yet the song, the song, the song—
it won't sleep quietly, so the boy who is

the boy I was still hears it. He spreads his wings;
he runs through the open door; his shoes fall from

the sky until snagged by their strings
by a wire sending a sweet girl's voice

from one home to another with an urgency that
a good man knows as a cry for help, not a song.

It's Important I Remember

THAT LOVE PRESUMES PROTECTION—

Maya says this, more or less, on the podcast in that voice of hers,
somehow managing sound without dislodging the clarity of silence,
and I sit in that slanted serenity for a while, thinking, dissolving
deduction by deduction down to the water that pools me person;
I peer inside myself and peep my face wrinkled by the ripples
of difficult questions stirring the soul to motion. I've long felt
I'm a lover, not a fighter. Only a man would think these separate
people. I learned how disappointing I can be in a moment of need;
it hit me less hard than her but hit me hard enough in the chest that
I've not caught my breath yet these years later, striking the same spot
where I still feel my mother's hand instilling discipline.
We settle in at
Mom's kitchen table and she tells my wife and me about the harassment
she endured on her job trying to feed four kids, targeted for her skin
and her skirt: Corporations are also people, also men who do nothing
except what they're not supposed to. Like the people who pay me,
I've thrown money at problems I'm part of, to help people post bail
or lawyer up, a lot of them making sixty-three cents to a white man's dollar.
I don't know if you've noticed all of them at the protests, cops at their front,
brothers at their back: It's a terrible place to be, in America or anywhere.

I read an article about one of them down in Tallahassee: Oluwatoyin Salau,
Toyin for short, strengthened by faith, a nineteen-year-old whose name means
God is worthy to be praised, who stomped the streets in George Floyd's
memory when she didn't have a safe address to return home to herself.
Sentences would be too much for my soft stomach, so I'll use fragments:

a church; an appeal; a man; a car ride; a shower; an █████; an escape;
a man; a car ride; a shower;
and again;
and again;
and again; gone.

The man who admitted to it, black, has the last name Glee, like exultant joy,
like to have taken from her and then also taken her life is more than a liking

we have inside us as with hoops or hip-hop, and I know that I almost let him get away even though I do not know him, that I'd be unable to identify him in a lineup where some are guilty and others are less guilty. The herstories have differences, but this more recent tragedy reminds me of Recy Taylor:

a church; a men; a car ride; an █████;
and again;
and again;
and again;
and again;
and again;
and again;
and again.

The day after the hearing, white vigilantes firebombed her house for having the gall to report anything at all in 1940s Alabama. Recy, her husband, and their daughter were forced to move in with Recy's father, Benny, back where Recy had grown up, and her father watched over the house at night from a tree with his shotgun loaded for any trouble that came.

The image comforts me in a sense, just how innocence does as a concept, as does forgiveness, as does redemption. But in this moment, what I ache to know is if he died up there in the branches of that tree. What I hurt to know is if it's love when you are protecting yourself at the same time. What I hope to know is if Benny could recognize trouble coming if it was as black as the glee in his daughter's face during her girlhood, not white like the glare of the headlights on the car that abducted her, and if he did recognize it, would he hesitate to shoot as I worry I would for how they looked much as I do: a brother.

It's Important I Remember

THAT HARRIET TUBMAN HAD A PISTOL ON HER AT ALL TIMES—

every time she crept across
the Maryland state line under moon cover.

The pistol had space for a single shot;
it had a singular purpose, a focus of aim.

Once the train had left their chains behind them,
there could be no turning back into what they were before;

the slave catchers never loomed as large a threat
as the stomach of an enslaved man turning like a pig on a spit.

If ever he tried to backslide, she'd have put the bullet in him
and kept northbound under starlight; after all,

rather than argue, she split town with several fugitives
and left her first husband to the life he said he wanted—

having returned intending his rescue, she found him married anew.
Seemingly a man of small devotion to vow or cause,

had he taken Harriet's hand at the offer, she probably would've
had to shoot him along the way to freedom,

though that act became a white man's pleasure years later.
But he didn't heed her, and her anger at the greatest betrayal

would've gone through another black man's back without hesitation
but with justification. And when someone stumbled

upon his breathless body in the wilderness, both corpse and compass
with his head pointed south, with his face stamping the mud—

when they rolled him over, I know
his face would be mine.

~~01.07.2023~~

sometimes it be your own peoples

It's Important I Remember
THAT BLACK MEN KILLED MALCOLM X—

and the devils who did it believed with every fiber of their
beings that white men were devils, as it was theologized, as it
was preached to them, very prominently at one point in time,
by the man they hollowed with a sawed-off shotgun and pistols
in front of his pregnant wife and young daughters, some goons
from the Newark temple, according to all the whispers, who smote
Ossie's shining black prince for sullying their prophet's reputation—
revealing he treated teenagers as women, then their love children as
nothing. For this they reduced the famously red-haired Sunni to rot,
a figure some felt could free their minds by his conviction alone if not,
one day, their onyx flesh, their ivory bones, their ruby blood like that
splattered across the ballroom stage. And all I have to say about this
avoidable tragedy is that, though dumb and destructive to the cause
of our collective liberation, the crime had at least been deliberated
beforehand in a smoke-filled room, that Brother Malcolm walked
everywhere he went up until that rostrum knowing what was going
to go down, that nobody else died that day who hadn't considered it
as casually as making a cup of coffee or setting down their house keys
where they could later find them on their way out the door.

In my lifetime, almost nobody I've heard of being killed
on a day-after-day cadence has had the privilege of assassination,
as crazy as that sounds to say; in the nineties and beyond it was and
is more a matter of who popped who when and where over what,
all of it ultimately small compared to the size of a cockroach's
dream of one day being considered beautiful. Gone—just *gone*.
Over Air Jordans or gold chains. Over commercial turf. Over lust
or radioactive ego. And the lie we've told ourselves is that Malcolm
died for our sakes, for freedom, when he, the reformed hoodlum, died for
utter foolishness with so much work left unfinished, unpublishable sans
his signature on the times. It hurts. It hurts so much to know some hand
is on the gun—a black one, a white one—and to pray for white because
the firearm is nonnegotiable for the kind of you that you are. That there,
my friend, is the Devil, is the grand design, is the shape of
six, six, six.

It's Important I Remember

THAT TUPAC SHAKUR WAS TWENTY-FIVE WHEN HE WAS MURDERED—

the Notorious B.I.G., Christopher Wallace, shot dead
one year younger less than one year later, also in a drive-by,

as if to mock how quickly any of us come and go, like this
pair of rich kids, all eyes on them, accidental luminaries

who were almost certainly not ready to die. Kids, I'll say
again: youthful people prone to bullshit and bad decisions.

I'm still growing into a beard my damn self and have already
surpassed both in longevity by several laps around the sun,

spinning with the planet like platinum records in disc changers that
represented their immortal souls for millions of fans. It didn't have

to end that way for them like it never really has to end that way
for anybody else. Forget the bicoastal beef, the recording booth

bravado, the subliminal and infamously explicit diss tracks:
None of that mess snatched them from their singular mothers.

What's often true yet unacknowledged is that a bullet can fill
a space that was already empty rather than making a space

in something that was whole. Pac was said by his homies to
have the loudest mouth, the hottest temper, but the biggest heart;

Biggie toted gats for years and talked a strong game but wasn't
close to being the most notorious gangster over in Brooklyn.

Even still, they died. Murdered for affiliations, as retaliation like
any other soulja in the streets. But there's little else one would

expect when black boys have to belong to something also.
If not to their country, and if not to a church, and if not to

their daddies, then to their chosen brothers who *man them up*,
who school them on everything manhood is supposed to buy

with no concern at whose expense. Power, pleasure: transacted
via posse. Thus the larger thing possesses the individual's will,

informs their actions almost to the point of demand—and so Pac
rides for Suge after getting bailed out of a sexual abuse sentence

that, in dream hampton's eyes, he wouldn't have faced if he stood
up to the thugs hanging onto him; Biggie Smalls has to call in

Crips for security whenever he goes-goes back-back to Cali-Cali.
The pistol cocked back before the pistol cocked back, as it

often does because a woman's genuine love is more attainable
than a man's—if a man's is attainable at all—and scarcity

is what drives value, what one shoots for, and not just figuratively.
This is what money meant to them whether they realized it or not.

In the moment the light flashed and the bass dropped to the floor;
their dear mamas probably never stood a chance, could never

have saved them when the fame and fortune already should've
accomplished the feat of salvation. As for me, still breathing

and still as black as an only chance, I'm simply longing to be
something rather than someone, though I've been less a different

case than them than I've been lucky. I put that on my mama—
while praying never the sound of a period in the pectoral.

It's Important I Remember

THAT JAY-Z ARRIVED ON THE DAY FRED HAMPTON DIED—

real niggas just multiply, he said, selling himself
to anybody that would buy the pursuit of billions as liberation work.

In saying this, Jay's mind slipped past Fred Hampton being
assassinated while his girlfriend Deborah slept next to him
eight months into carrying their child, a baby boy to be named Fred.

That's *real* real nigga multiplication.
Fred knew the streets like Jay,
but Jay didn't know the streets like Fred.
That's real, my nigga.

See, what caught Fred two in the dome from CPD
were the disputes he could smooth over between deadly adversaries,
so gifted with the gab he got white boys mobbing
with blacks and the Latinx, so good even Jesse Jackson jocked
his rainbow steelo as signifier and testament.

"Dead Presidents II" comes to mind for me suddenly—
when Jigga declares divine intervention for three bullets
passing him by. And maybe it was. And maybe God,
like most things, looks whiter in juxtaposition, but whatever.

Tell Hov the poor can still help the poor if they're one;
reach *a billy* first for what if it ain't a club
you're going to swing at heads with?

We say we're not going to fight capitalism with black capitalism,
or Fred said, rather, speaking on behalf of a fist of people—
and Jay dropped nary a bar in response but
draped Fred's name like a king's robe over his brushed-off shoulders.

I remember when Kaepernick was still out of a gig and
Mr. Carter cashed that Goodell check because he knew it was good
even if not underwritten with good intentions,
pro-black in the sense of demonstrating a profit.

Getting rich and giving back was supposed to be the win-win
for he and we; he gave only game back if anything
and charged $9.99 for it when most of us
ain't even trying to play no more.

It's Important I Remember

THAT TWISTA CAN MAKE YOU A CELEBRITY OVERNIGHT—

if you rub him right, hand to belly, "wax on, wax off" motions.
His velour jumpsuit will turn blue; he's a friend you've never had
the likes of before. Twista will make you famous by snapping a finger.
Twista will fill mouths with your name from the left molars to the right.
Twista will play something the people like; will pick the right whip for you
he knows they'll like; will give you ice to give out like Kobe gave his wife.
Twista will make you a prince or the local equivalent. America doesn't
have a throne yet, so the closest thing is the *Resolute* desk; Twista
will make you the president against all pundit predictions. Twista
will make you somebody all those little somebodies out there
can't trust but no doubt will, even a few of the black ones—
third eyes open—who profess to never trust a damn thing.

It's Important I Remember

THAT KANYE WEST DOESN'T CARE ABOUT BLACK PEOPLE—

as it turns out, Mike Myers, the man behind the international man of mystery, hadn't seen a ghost but had seen the future, standing there, face strained by surprise on a live telecast for Hurricane Katrina relief. Nobody asked him what he saw because we know what we saw ourselves: That any president, let alone a Republican serving in the wake of Nixon and Reagan, could leave black people under siege of water, drowning or starved skinny, wasn't a surprising thought, but to hear it spoken publicly was, at that time, during a four-year pandemic of patriotism, absolutely bold. Boldness has never been in doubt when it comes to Ye, not then and not since— the epitome of *strong mind meets big mouth*. As self-conscious as I was in those days, nerdy and past due on my pubescent growth spurt, there was no way I couldn't be taken with him, high off crack music and whatnot. I loved the old Kanye because I thought he loved me, loved us, like he loved his mama, like his mama loved books he'll never read. We saw what happened after she transitioned, 'twas like Shakespearean tragedy adapted for the gossip blogs. I think back to the towering waters after the storm surge and to the dryness of the land beneath his eyes since maternal separation and I know something is broken, deeply broken, when he's sitting down in the Oval Office with the president of the United States, the one that came after the one more people would've guessed, but there's a beef there that the two men on opposite sides of the desk share about the man who last held the office, though the stakes of that steak are not the same and never could be. Instead of a teddy bear, we find a sheep in a baseball cap; come to find out, free thinking not aimed toward freedom is a waste of a thought. He rambles earnestly but strays from poetry while the camera flashes in his eyes, eyes that absorb the light but reflect the president's orange glimmer back to him like praise. This sight would've seemed impossible in 2005, but so many things assumed to have changed by then turned out to have been the same the whole time. When Yeezus said, *Slavery was a choice*, his lips were quotation marks followed by no attribution, puckered insults insinuating that his own people provided no friction against their reassignment as property, as ornaments of wealth and power. The irony of the scene is regrettable, straight-up sad: Enslaved people built the damn White House and he's acting like he's finally *made it*, hey Mama— not seeing how seamlessly he blends into the walls with all the other bodies bearing the load of imperial lunacy, forcibly upholding, even and especially in their death, the supremacy of a violent orientation on the orbit of the world, reinforcing the kinds of ideas that spin sound heads silly as the slope of history slickens with blood.

It's Important I Remember

THAT THE OBAMAS' FIRST DATE WAS SEEING *DO THE RIGHT THING*—

a Spike Lee joint.   An imperative statement

in one's own voice   spoken in the attic of an ache.

This is not the type of movie   people talk through,

so they say nothing at all.   When Radio Raheem is choked to death

by the police   in front of Sal's Famous Pizzeria,

Barack does not   so much as whimper. Michelle

squirms in her seat   as if a ghost combed through her hair.

Mookie shatters   the window to tears with a garbage can.

A forehead wrinkles   in thought, barely

visible in the theater's   hushed blue complexion.

After the credits roll,   they roll out, sharing a ride

slowed by the weight   of contemplation on old axles.

Wheels are turning   in ovals.

They know what they are   preparing for even

if they do not.   The two of them leave

an impression on the film   in my mind,

which becomes this poem   and its silences.

It's Important I Remember

THAT I'M AVOIDING THE FOOTAGE—

purposefully. But I imagine it
looked like this—

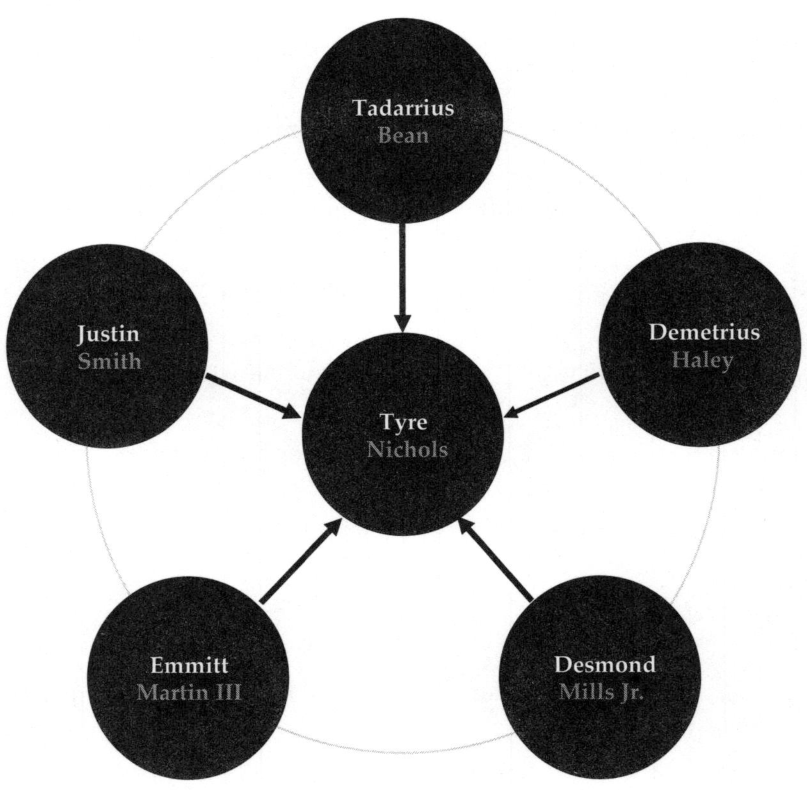

I imagine it
looked like safety
should by the shape of it, the shade.
                                                            It should have
touched us like a twilight beheld by the sentimental eye—
that moment when the officers raised the son who'd
fallen off his skateboard to his feet
and sent him on his way home.   I imagine it
                                                        so that it is,   so that it becomes what was.

It's Important I Remember

THAT PARTING IS SUCH SWEET SORROW—

that is, they were star-crossed
beneath the spangled banner:
Bayard Rustin and his buddy, Martin.

That is, they were double-crossed
by blackness like what
visibles starlight in the sky.

That is, Martin was the shining star
of the movement, the face
held over all the other black faces
like a mask for masquerade,
and Bayard was standing by, working
the stage lights and keeping schedule.

That is, the stage had been set
for a full-on demonstration
at the 1960 DNC in Los Angeles,
and parts were to be played
in the political theater.

That is, Adam Clayton Powell Jr.,
Harlem's congressman, created the conflict
that pushed the plot forward.

That is, the plot was an actual plan
hatched of dramatic antagonism
to prevent slippage of power
from congressional halls to the streets.

That is, the threat of the legislator's lie
divided love asymmetrically
between person and people.

That is, Bayard loved the people
more than his own person
and Martin was a person people
loved more than themselves,
though evidenced as reciprocal.

That is, there is a love
that touched them both
and a love that didn't touch
in the way the lie would
tell it to the press.

That is, one love was dangerous
to established factions
and one love was dangerous
to established factions.

That is, Bayard faced
the fact of the past
and Martin faced
the fiction of the future.

That is, the present became
an instance of fissure
that surfaced pained feelings.

That is, the sudden feeling
surrounding Martin was
that Bayard should step away
from the production
of civil disobedience
as part of their esteemed troupe.

That is, the show had to go on
at the party convention,
across the entire country—
but some actors aren't replaceable.

That is, it turned out to be
more of a pause than
a permanent departure, but
one man swallowed pride
while the other swallowed poison.

That is, this saga wasn't wholly
determinative of either man's fate,
though, as in *Romeo and Juliet*,
one died before the other,
who was left behind with
a kind of longing in his heart
as two stars shot past one another
without touching in a way these men
never did, like the legislator's lie
would've alleged.

It's Important I Remember

THAT ONE BLACK JUSTICE REPLACED ANOTHER—

Thurgood Marshall, whose name echoes in the ear
like virtue itself from a church bell,

sequeled on the Supreme Court of the United States by

Clarence Thomas, whose name slips too easily
into a literary allusion that men like my uncles
spit on in disgust.

One Southern president's appointment succeeded
one Southern president's appointment;

a Texan's right to choose gave way to
a Texan's right to choose.

His glasses and robe;
his glasses and robe.

How the circumstances touch is nearly sensual, as much
as what occurs on the other side of a bedroom door; it elicits
expectation, and I can't accurately express to you the level
of disappointment in knowing the dastardly plan worked
so well for the powers that be trying to disenfranchise us, that
voucher and charter the schools separate again and genuflect
to the same text that forbade us being beings of dignity.

The twenty-four years between their Senate confirmations
is a shorter distance than my mother ran to give birth to me,
just one decision she made of many; that second black
justice has been around three decades now, long enough
to install a second Bush as president and nullify equal
access to the ballot and re-redesignate half
the population as purely a vessel for the other.

Under our system of government, I know the hill he will die on
is Capitol Hill, the name *Anita* dangling from his bottom lip
inside a strand of saliva.
When he stands at the pearly gates,
I believe it will be his predecessor prosecuting his unworthiness
for admission to a kinder court. Justice, as it always does, will
have come too late—but its robe will be black in color; it will be
black in creed.

~~11.07.2020~~

the thing with feathers

It's Important I Remember

THAT A LACK OF IMAGINATION KILLS—

truth be told.

The last time you called for help, you didn't phone the police;

you dialed up

your neighbor. There should be no doubts: It should always be

fireworks that

you hear. The gate doesn't keep them out so much as keep you in,

like a sheep.

A door is a door when it dances on its weary hinges; otherwise,

it's only wall.

Home is bigger than a house; it's much easier to give away the

smaller thing.

The woman you teach to fish can then fish with you. Jesus healed

the sick just

because they were sick. Violence is the answer to violence, but

violence isn't

the answer to the original question. Before our laws, there was a

natural order:

We settled on bad designs, but boxes are to be thought a way out of.

It's Important I Remember

THAT THERE'S ALWAYS HOPE—

you can still see the faint torch.

I come from the fire city
amid rumors of death.

You know the stories. You were raised on them,

raise your small voice against
any kind of mother.

Fight the urge to rattle off statistics.
Distrust everything.

I am not done with my changes.

Keep moving through time and I will finally arrive

piece by piece: The body prayers home

through halls of cloud
in the dark, reaching for you.

Eventually something catches,

rage and calm join,

life bends down and kisses.

We encounter each other in
faithfulness to the light.

I mean to tell you everywhere I go,

sing you home into yourself and back to reason:

You do not have to ***be*** *good;*
that doesn't mean you ***aren't*** *good.*

You say you think I have courage—

It's my turn.

Watch the moon eat the sun.

What's going on   is going on.

The hour of lead.

The plural of *dust*.

Between good and evil, I was so sure good would win.

A pattern that others made *may* prevail in the world:
One thing was like another thing and that thing like another.

When despair for the world grows in me
my fingers close around   flight.

It's okay to write   *I deserve—*

my one hand holding tight.

Hold on, because the poets are still alive—

we are, I am, you are—
in the strenuous briefness.

There are days we live as if death was nowhere in the background.

There is laughter every day in the terrible streets.

We are remarkably loud. Not masked. Rough

matches against so much gasoline.

Go firmly to the window and listen
into the pane that proves the world is a cold, smooth place

for the ghosts to walk through.

It *is* you I am addressing:

So much disappearing goes on unregistered.

I did not hear it though I clearly mouthed *poor thing, poor thing.*

I take the elevator and go down
into the darkness that is the mind of the day.

I'm grieving. I'm very busy remembering

reality is what it is— this— suffering—

that force of present absence
still unstoried, artless.

The closer I get, the more "I" recedes:

sorrow as *the other.*

We were made to understand it.

We have memorized America. How it was born.

Some fool themselves into believing, but I know what I know
and drank to remember to forget.

I forget things, too. It makes me sad.

The photograph halted them in life and now keeps them.

I change grip and the image fades,
loosening the philosophical knot of why.

After the night goes to sleep,
the horizon leans forward

as if I need to be told what's white and what isn't.

The mental optics rove.

I sing through the struggle.

Just blackness I could live on.

I can't help thinking of thanks.

Many have brought the gifts I use
apparelled in celestial light, the glory and the freshness.

The sun filtered through
my little bones.

I woke up *and it was.*

Make the world say what you want:

Visible the scale of imagination.

So many birds here is what I was trying to say.

Around the corner I could see
my face, your face, millions of faces in morning's mirrors.

We say our own names.

I cannot tell anymore when a door opens or closes.
I don't know how to sit still or move without purpose.

Brightness in the eye,
I am practicing good,
grow larger— a kind of power surviving.

I pledge allegiance to laughter
moved through the gap in my teeth like birdsong,

the only animal who smiles with his lips,

the color of balloons.

I was raised by a beautiful man.

When you suffer, I suffer—

best to start again—

run like light—

do what has to be done—   again.

I am programmed to this language,
these last strands of man in me.

Something in you believes   that it is not the end.

Who can see this and not?

a cento, with ninety-nine thank yous and one pat on the back

It's Important I Remember
THAT GOD INTERVENES—

intravenously—

a metronomic trickle into your bloodstream,

the consciousness racing back

to your heart—that old organ with a new pedal.

Too often it takes seeing death up close to see life.

Maybe the nine-millimeter missed by millimeters;

perhaps the bag around the bones dried up how grapes do

because the planet is fevering us away.

Believe: *You saw what you saw*;

light likes to shoot straight through

instead of curl around a container of identity.

You see how you see now: The room you've awoken to

is white in its noises and walls and that

decidedly disquiets the variant of you that has returned

from the other side of violence.

After the Lord has made another day,

it's your turn, my sibling in tenderness;

and on what would be your seventh day of making, you rest

on the porch with a pitcher sweating its sugar out

while you watch children bicycle by

unsupervised, unafraid.

~~01.06.2021~~

to be determined

It's Important

THAT THE MAJORITY OF AMERICANS AGREE

that democracy is the best system of government

that people should voice their views without fear of reprisal

that there needs to be police reform

that racism and discrimination are bad

that students shouldn't be taught whitewashed history

that the country benefits from the presence of immigrants

that legislation should be passed to protect Dreamers

that the country has been a force for good in the world

that high achievement should be expected of all people

that a person's gender needn't conform to their biological sex

that affordable housing is a problem where they live

that their neighbors are not their friends

that the courts have become too political

that America is not perfect

I Remember

THE COUNTRY IS ON THE WRONG TRACK—

that democracy is under threat

that government can monitor our activities without warrants

that it can be necessary to sacrifice freedoms to fight terrorism

that calling all white people racist is not fair

that students shouldn't be made to feel guilty due to their race

that a system is needed to decide who can enter the country

that America is in danger of losing its cultural identity

that it is acceptable to work with autocrats if it protects us

that there are underlying differences between men and women

that athletes should compete according to their biological sex

that to be a true American you must believe in capitalism

that there is diminishing civility in politics

that to be a true American you must believe in God

that America is the greatest country on earth

It's Important I Remember

THAT DONALD TRUMP'S SUPPORTERS ATTACKING THE CAPITOL WAS UNPRECEDENTED, NOT UNPREDICTABLE—

because I, for one, *could* believe what I was witnessing unfold like a letter written on executive stationery tucked in a drawer of the *Resolute* desk. My right knee, which was once my great-grandmother's knee, had been acting up for days, weeks maybe, foretelling storm. In my sleepless mind, I misplaced the word for *the happening of lightning and thunder without bringing rain* and now have only clumsier language at my disposal, an American's English. I shed no tears for my country as they scaled the walls and steps, breached the building by busting windows, the mob's flags slapping in the icy breeze like tongues that know nothing of consequences.

The US flag.
The Confederate flag.
The Trump 2020 flag.

They stormed the Capitol to bring about a reign that, with no doubt in my mind, would rain blood. *Trump Is King*, the troll messaged me on the blue bird app a month before this all went down; I don't worry whether it was a human being or a bot because there's no fundamental difference in the underlying programming.

The point is this: I don't believe in kings. I believe in the Lord.

But God doesn't have to believe in anything, and so here we are: one nation going under with a watching eye above it all, as beheld on the back of a dollar bill.

Simply put, an ellipse is an oval.

One can create an ellipse, geometrically speaking, by slicing an inclined plane through a cone.

A cone like a dunce cap is a cone.

A cone like Pinocchio's nose is a cone.

A hallmark of American political campaigns is the comedic or satiric depiction of one candidate by the supporters of another. I've seen the sitting president of the United States drawn up wearing a dunce cap and diaper, a swipe at his perceived lack of intelligence and impulsivity. I've seen the sitting president of the United States depicted with Pinocchio's nose, a swipe at his rampant and relentless dishonesty.

Today, that undeniable dunce, that pathological liar, stepped out of the Oval Office and onto the oval field to address his supporters, parkland known as the Ellipse. Hours from now, this will be pinpointed as the moment of incitement, but that flame-stoking has, truthfully, been happening for months, for years, for decades at the pace of an artery clogging from overconsumption of red meat.

Another name for an ellipse is an ellipsis.

The order to attack isn't explicitly made but, instead, implied; careful omissions augment the president's plausible deniability.

A cone of silence has descended over the speaker and crowd, like in an episode of *Get Smart*. Everyone outside the plexiglass bubbles, each shaped similarly to how the Capitol dome happens to be, understands the president's speech for what it is.

I must admit, evil does have a subtle kind of intelligence that impresses me as much as it terrifies me—how easily it's let to pass as stupid or insignificant or even meaning no harm at all.

February 2021

Robert A. Pape, a political science professor at the University of Chicago, writes in *The Atlantic* that of the 193 individuals charged in connection with the January 6 insurrection thus far, 89 percent "have no connection to existing far-right militias, white-nationalist gangs, or other established violent organizations."

On average, the indicted parties are roughly forty years old. Four in ten own their own business or hold down a white-collar job: doctors, lawyers, accountants, you name it. Fewer than ten people for every hundred is unemployed, idle as a threat.

It turns out over half the insurrectionists in this sample came from counties that Biden won during the 2020 election.

Demographically, these vandals were not the young men marching through Charlottesville with tiki torches who vowed that the Jews would not replace them and ran over Heather Heyer with a car for daring to counterbalance their bigotry. There is no "epidemic of loneliness" for these folks to hide their grotesque deeds behind.

These are your neighbors.

They are my neighbors.

Pathology, chiefly, studies the causes and effects of diseases.
Pathology can, alternatively, refer to abnormality in a social context.

Personally, I find normal people to be the deadliest—as stealthy as influenza during the era of the novel coronavirus.

I'll concede that I have no great sympathy for the police, the FBI, or any other US intelligence agency. You can put that down in black ink. I could list the reasons why and they'd all be the names of real people who were killed or jailed on the flimsiest of evidence. Nonetheless, you told me, once upon a time or two or three, that blue lives matter and a distant part of me, unwittingly, had listened.

That cop crushed between the Capitol doors was on your side until you said he wasn't. Blue turned to black in the flash of a camera.

Who is protected and who is served?
Whose law must be upheld? Whose order?

Ashli Babbitt, a veteran of the United States Air Force, was killed by a Capitol police officer's bullet after failing to comply with his orders to fall back from the doors leading to the House of Representatives. The shooting was captured on video.

I blame her for her own death, reversing my usual stance in this scenario. I'm not disturbed by my admission, but I recognize the irony. Maybe I relish being in this position of judgment, for once, and that makes me potentially unreliable, not as a witness but as a person.

The officer who shot Ms. Babbitt—Lieutenant Michael Byrd—asserts that by doing what he did that day, he saved countless lives; I take it that he means the lives of members of Congress and his fellow law enforcement officers. By another interpretation, he saved my life also, I who was only there as a specter of all that the mob hates.

You can put that down in ink, black.

One of the funniest scenes I saw in the immediate aftermath of the insurrection was a white man losing his shit in the airport for not being allowed to board a flight from Charlotte to Denver. It was his whining that amused me. *They kicked me off the plane. They called me a fucking terrorist. And they want to fucking ruin my life.* Like a small child, he seemed surprised that his actions brought about a reaction. As the internet likes to say, he fucked around and found out . . . that if you don't wear a mask on the plane, American Airlines will refuse to let you board, per company policy.

This is what they do to us, he screamed. That was on January 8, two short days after American democracy was, maybe, mortally wounded.

The video title on YouTube reads "Trump supporter learns they're on the no-fly list at AIRPORT after storming the Capitol, FREAKS OUT." The title of the video doesn't need to be accurate in letter to be true in sentiment.

Calls from Congress to place arrested insurrectionists on no-fly lists by TSA and the FBI followed in the days immediately after January 6, but such a task takes time to be completed. Punishment is swift only for citizens flying second class. Correction: Punishment is swift only for second-class citizens.

On January 20, two weeks after his supporters sacked the Capitol, Donald Trump flew to Mar-a-Lago on Air Force One, disgraced in a modest majority of eyes but replete with all luxuries and privileges of the office he refused to relinquish.

The presidential plane flew back to Washington without him onboard, but his Secret Service detail stayed behind alongside him, standing guard around him because he remains an important person to the country, or something like that.

In my day we used to █████ *presidents*, she said. I'll leave the quote unattributed, but let's just say this is a woman who's seen some things in her life, had a lot to live through: survived the Deep South, survived the Great Migration, survived a husband.

I recognize the joke in what she spoke as well as its opposite, the shadow behind every unit of alphabet that makes it look bold against blank paper.

President Kennedy died a relatively young man, and Lee Harvey Oswald died at half his age.

I'm old. I've lived a long life. I could take one for the team—a joke with too much truth in it to laugh. Being deadly honest, she doesn't have it in her (and never would). A hate of hate itself isn't strong enough to pull off a crime of such magnitude, the will already weakened by the conscience.

To kill for a cause, you must be willing to die for it, and the pacemaker betrays her heart on the matter. Kindness will have to do the despicable deed for her, but kindness never kills.

October 2023

Ever curious, I scour the FBI's online Crime Data Explorer after encountering a headline stating hate crimes have increased in the latest 2022 dataset. It's light work for me: I swim in spreadsheets daily and rarely come up for air; at times I ask the numbers to lie to me, but they refuse because they aren't politicians.

More than half of reported hate crimes in the United States are committed against a specific race or ethnicity, with most of those incidents being classified as antiblack. The number of antiblack incidents has increased since the previous year, per my calculations.

Anti-Jewish crimes: +36% vs. 2021
Anti–Native American or anti–Alaskan Native crimes: +35% vs. 2021
Anti-trans crimes: +35% vs. 2021

Antigay crimes are up. Anti-Hispanic or -Latino crimes, up. Anti-Muslim crimes, up.

A rising tide (of hate) lifts all boats (on blood).

There's concern being broadcast that Israel's bombardment of Gaza will blow back against Jewish Americans, release pent up antisemitism. It isn't wrong to worry for my friends in synagogues, just as it isn't wrong to worry for my friends in mosques; my country is my country, after all.

The White House briefing room press release reads *Hate never goes away, it only hides.*

I jump back into the FBI database. Every year, between 1991 and 2022, black people are the most-targeted group for hate crimes in the United States, as a percentage of reported incidents, well ahead of their share of the population. For three decades, the top of the list never changes. Some hate, as evidenced, doesn't hide very well.

Any hate crime is a stain on the soul of America, says the White House.

Some stains never come out, says the poet. *In that case, you must throw the garment away.*

Who were you on January 6?
Who were you on January 7?

Who were you on September 11?
Who were you on September 12?

Who were you on October 7?
Who were you on October 8?
Who were you on October 9?
Who were you on October 10?
Who were you on October 11?
Who were you on October 12?
Who were you on October 13?
Who were you on October 14?
Who were you on October 15?
Who were you on October 16?
Who were you on October 17?
Who were you on October 18?
Who were you on October 19?
Who were you on October 20?
Who were you on October 21?
Who were you on October 22?
Who were you on October 23?
Who were you on October 24?
Who were you on October 25?
Who were you on October 26?
Who were you on October 27?
Who were you on October 28?
Who were you on October 29?
Who were you on October 30?
Who were you for Halloween?

Where were you on January 6?

Were you American? Were you
Native or African American?

Were you a patriot? Were you a parrot?

Did they pull the blanket over your cage
to ease you into slumber and away from speaking?

When tyranny came, how
peacefully did you sleep?

Did you ever wake up?

I think the kids are going to be all right, sleeping
in their hastily pitched tents.
                                        The weather is warming with the season
even before one considers the heat of national media attention
against their napes.
                              Gaza is all but gone yet they don't want
anyone using the word *genocide*.
                                              The students sit shiva in a sense
on their campuses, innocent by the most conservative interpretations
but complicit through taxation for the continuation of catastrophe
in occupied Palestine.
                                  University presidents call police in to control
the unwanted crowd; precedent holds the injuries that followed—
who they belonged to and who inflicted them—were predictable
whereas the fact of who made the phone calls was disappointing
and deadly for the prospects of a free society.

                Another November election looms:

Our aspiring tyrant has returned to electoral preeminence
and plans to dislodge his detested successor who ships out
humanitarian aid that's only necessary because of a different
tyrant that he underwrites.
                                              Alas, evil rigs the vote yet again,
steals the practice from the cold grip of the theory.
                                                                  Somewhere,
I'm sure, there's democracy—
                                          in an encampment the cops are bulldozing
as they were trained to by the world's most brutal officers, the same world
wobbling on an axis of power, power that's supposed to go to the people
by social contract, to the earnest youth voting who tilt the outcomes of our
political pageants at the margins, the kids who so clearly aren't all right
with any of this.
                              How power punches downward. How it brings
military against meager militia; American bombs upon babies in incubators.

The American president is, at once, head of government and head of state. The officeholder, in that sense, is unitary—the pinnacle of American power and identity enveloped within one person. In that respect, the American president sounds a lot like a king.

On Sunday nights, my beloved and I take in a popular television series based on a fantasy book; during its first season, the sensible king we were introduced to deteriorated into something unrecognizable and incoherent before dying and leaving a power struggle between two sides of his family. This season, the blood and the fire are flying from long swords and dragons. What fascinates me about this fantastical world is its complicated and winding history, its absolutist politics.

For several months now, there have been worries that the current American president is too old to continue on to a second term: He has slowed in speech, softened in voice, lost the plot on the debate stage and during interviews several times.

Where the show I'm watching appears to be headed is the plunge of a kingdom into widespread violence and disarray, the rise of despots who delight in their lack of enlightenment. We small folk have worries because we have tenuous lives, and that's why we look for escapes like television shows where our analogues are massacred and forgotten.

In our own world, there's a man who breathes fire like a dragon that will burn everything to the ground, who will gladly rule over the ashes of his kingdom. There's a panel of judges who assert the American president is, in legality, the American king, who sits on a gunmetal throne above the law. The current president still thinks he's a president, however. He's in visible and natural decline, given his age, which means he's also in denial. He believes he's the hero in this story, swiping back at concerns raised about his fragile candidacy that stem from worrying over our fragile lives should the worst man claim that office.

We reached the end of the first season with an unshakeable feeling in our stomachs that the next wouldn't be nearly as good.

The throne will play its games with us; the dragon will burn our houses down whenever he wants. Witness American power. Witness American identity. Our king is a lot like a president whose chains have been removed, what linked them to the little people.

July 13, 2024

I just received the text message: Out in Pennsylvania, somebody took a shot at the man who once said he could shoot someone on Fifth Avenue and not lose a single vote. The former president survived the attempt but suffered a wound to his right ear.

In real time, as the developing story unfolds into a map of our societal collapse, I follow the path of the attempted assassin's bullet through online echo chambers: *The radical left is out of control. I bet Biden is behind this. What a disgusting display of violence. We have to come together.* I'm bouncing an unwell baby on my knee, watching the news networks loop video of the shooting, the ending always the same with that (admittedly) great showman being lifted to his feet by Secret Service agents, raising his fist in the air while the American flag waves above as they hurry him into the vehicle readied to rush him to the hospital.

A picture like that is worth a thousand silences from your adversaries; most strongmen in history would have to stage a photo that good.

I want to know who fired those shots. I want to know why they did it. I want to know where they're from, what they look like, who they claim to represent. I want to know how scared I should be of reprisals. I want to know, for sure, that it's better they missed their mark.

The FBI doesn't identify the assailant publicly until after midnight: twenty-year-old kid, registered Republican, raised in a conservative household, loner, gun enthusiast, Pennsylvania resident. I release a sigh of relief how I always do when a crime cannot be blamed on me. But, ultimately, they bury the lede by morning, downplay the would-be assassin's profile and assert the authorities have no motive they're able to report yet. I suppose it's fine, since it doesn't matter much anyway. The resurrection has already happened.

It's not exactly true that Trump became a martyr that day: Any person worthy of that mantle is dead. Rather, I believe that the former president became something more, something beyond even the office he covets: Donald Trump transformed into the cause that martyrs will die for. On a random Saturday in July, I'm not sure I witnessed a god intervene to prevent a tragedy so much as saw a god be invented with a nation now solidly underneath him, astonished, shocked into an allegiance with great intensity and that will never be earned.

The aging American president resigned himself to reality, stepped away from his reelection effort to endorse his second-in-command, a woman both black and brown in origin, who stood a better chance at beating the brazen bigot. I'll remember this day forever, assuming, that is, I don't lose my mind along the way to whatever feels like victory but is a falsehood made of chicken feathers.

What needs to be determined is if this was the beginning of the end or if it was the end of the beginning. The ink is still wet, as is the blood in my veins, but one day both will have to dry.

I rebuke you in the name of Jesus, Sonya Massey said to the police, *I'm sorry, I'm sorry*, and then she said nothing ever again. I'm supposed to be feeling hopeful right now, for we have found, perhaps, a formidable challenger to the fascist presidential ticket. And, indeed, something tickles me inside like a sunray within a windowpane at daybreak. It makes me sick to my stomach to smile and genuinely mean it; I'm utterly hysterical while a former prosecutor is enveloped in political hysteria. In supposedly unprecedented times, the one precedent left undisturbed is that we will die without even the tiniest shred of dignity afforded to us. Killed—it must be argued, up to this point in our country's sordid history—democratically. As an outcome of public policy that has survived administration after administration, those that were decidedly hostile and, also, those that were supposedly staffed with friends.

Please don't be too nice.

Any guy that can do a body slam, he's my kind of guy.

Can't you just shoot them? Just shoot them in the legs or something?

When the looting starts, the shooting starts.

No, they're not humans, they're not humans, they're animals.

We could fix Portland in, I would say, forty-five minutes.

I will deploy the United States military and quickly solve the problem.

That's the way it has to be.

There has to be retribution.

You'll never take back our country with weakness.

Our country has been under siege for a long time.

We will root out the communists, Marxists, fascists, and the radical left thugs—

vermin within the confines of our country.

In 2016, I declared: I am your voice.

Today, I add: I am your warrior.

I am your justice.

And for those who have been wronged and betrayed, I am your retribution.

We're going to walk down to the Capitol.

Remember this day forever.

On January 20, in the year of our Lord 2025, they will head to the Capitol wearing their hallmark red hats: by train, plane, automobile, and foot. They will ignite into cheers when he steps through the double doors and descends the platform steps, flanked by dignitaries who worship and fear him how no mortal should be worshipped or feared. In the antithesis of poetry, a man referred to as the chief justice will lead him through a sacred oath—right hand to God, left on the Bible—and he will assume the office of the presidency once again. Thereafter, he will proceed to make the oath meaningless. He will keep only the promises he made behind closed doors. He will reign rather than preside and, I envision, doves will fall dead from the sky, silver bullets still inside their bodies.

I don't know if "America" will survive, but I know that we will.

Alisha B. Wormsley already pronounced there are black people in the future. Not possibly, not probably—definitely. Black women don't lie about their survival. Black women survive.

It's been said that history is written by the winners.

There are black people in the future talking to black people in the present, just as there are black people in the present talking to black people in the past.

What is being attempted against us has failed already, is failing now, will fail then.

Only books that have already been written can be banned.

The future is history that hasn't happened yet, so there can be no refusal to teach it.

So much can be learned about what will be then even now, *habibi*. *Hermano*. *Comrade*.

My nigga, it's important that you and I remember we've already won.

There are   black people   in the future
descended from   black people   in the present
descended from   black people   in the past

who resisted. Who rebelled. Who rewrote
the sentence they gave us.

03.11.2020 • The World Health Organization officially declares COVID-19 a global pandemic.

01.20.2017 • Donald Trump is inaugurated as the forty-fifth president of the United States in a peaceful transition of power from the administration of President Barack Obama, the nation's first Black president.

06.01.2020 • Amid nationwide protests in response to the murder of George Floyd by Minneapolis police, President Donald Trump clears demonstrators from the area near Lafayette Park in Washington, DC, with tear gas for the purpose of staging a photo op at St. John's Church to promote himself as "the president of law and order."

01.27.2017 • President Donald Trump signs an executive order that bans entry into the United States for individuals from several predominantly Muslim countries while suspending refugee admissions for 120 days. The executive order is swiftly challenged in court.

08.20.1619 • The first Africans brought to the (British) American colonies as property arrive at Point Comfort, located in modern-day Hampton, Virginia. Their arrival allowed for chattel slavery to take root in what would eventually become the United States of America, although other enslaved Black people were present in Spanish-controlled territories that would also later become American domain.

06.17.2021 • Juneteenth, an African American cultural celebration, becomes a federal holiday. The holiday commemorates the emancipation of enslaved African Americans and falls on the anniversary of Union Major General Gordon Granger ordering the final enforcement of President Abraham Lincoln's Emancipation Proclamation in Texas on June 19, 1865, two months after the conclusion of the American Civil War and over two years after Lincoln's proclamation was initially issued.

05.25.2020 • George Floyd, an unarmed Black man, is killed by a Minneapolis police officer via asphyxiation. The murder is captured on video. Floyd is seen to have made his physical distress known to the officer, who does not heed his pleas.

09.17.1787 • The final draft of the US Constitution is signed in Philadelphia, Pennsylvania, scrapping the Articles of Confederation and creating a more powerful federal government.

11.08.2016 • Real estate mogul and reality TV star Donald Trump, the Republican nominee for president of the United States in the 2016 presidential election, defeats former Secretary of State Hillary Clinton, the Democratic nominee, who had been favored to win the race.

01.05.2021 • The Georgia senatorial runoff election is held to determine the balance of power in the US Senate. After the votes are counted over the next few days, Democrats Raphael Warnock and Jon Ossoff defy decades of history by defeating their Republican opponents. This victory grants Democrats effective control of the Senate in addition to the House of Representatives and the White House. In the press, the win is largely attributed to the organizing work of former State Representative Stacey Abrams—an African American woman—and is delivered on the back of high turnout and margins among African American women.

06.13.2020 • Oluwatoyin Salau, a nineteen-year-old activist from Tallahassee, Florida, is found murdered, as is seventy-five-year-old Victoria Sims. Both were involved in local politics. They were murdered by Aaron Glee Jr., a Black man from Orlando, Florida. Glee also confessed to raping Salau.

01.07.2023 • Tyre Nichols is beaten to death by a group of five African American police officers in Memphis, Tennessee. Nichols's death leads to another surge in protests against ongoing state-sanctioned violence, which disproportionately victimizes Black people.

11.07.2020 • After four days of counting votes, former Vice President Joe Biden is declared the winner of the 2020 US presidential election, defeating the incumbent, President Donald Trump. He is to become the forty-sixth president of the United States.

01.06.2021 • Incited to insurrection by President Donald Trump, a mass of demonstrators storm the US Capitol, attempting to stop the counting of electoral votes that would constitutionally certify former Vice President Joe Biden's victory in the 2020 presidential election (and thus keep the incumbent in power). Four people die during the insurrection, and the grounds of the Capitol are defaced and damaged. Vice President Mike Pence and members of Congress are targeted by many who breach the building, but they escape physical harm.

IMPORTANT NOTES

"IT'S IMPORTANT I REMEMBER THAT THERE ARE SEVERAL WAYS TO KILL HOUSEPLANTS—" makes use of a popular phrase among protesters ("they tried to bury us, they didn't know we were seeds") that traces its introduction into English from a translation of the Greek poet Dinos Christianopoulos. The quote originates from the collection *The Body and the Wormwood*, translated by Nicholas Kostis. The original couplet reads, per Kostis's translation, "what didn't you do to bury me / but you forgot that I was a seed."

"IT'S IMPORTANT I REMEMBER THAT *DARKNESS* AND *BLACKNESS* AREN'T PERFECT SYNONYMS—" references eight minutes and forty-six seconds, the length of the initial phone-recorded bystander video of George Floyd's murder by officer Derek Chauvin on May 25, 2020, in Minneapolis, Minnesota. This number was commonly used as a battle cry in public demonstrations in the immediate wake of Floyd's death. The bystander video begins with Chauvin's knee on Floyd's neck. Body-cam footage later released showed that Floyd was actually asphyxiated for nine minutes and twenty-nine seconds, and this number was cited in Chauvin's trial.

"IT'S IMPORTANT I REMEMBER THAT THINGS ARE GETTING BACK TO NORMAL AROUND HERE—" was, in part, inspired by the murder of Jordan Neely by former US Marine Daniel Penny on the New York City subway on May 1, 2023.

"IT'S IMPORTANT I REMEMBER THAT THERE WAS NO POET AT DONALD TRUMP'S INAUGURATION—" quotes two selections from Federico García Lorca's lecture "Theory and Play of the Duende," delivered in 1933.

"IT'S IMPORTANT I REMEMBER THAT A TANK HAS NEVER STOPPED THE LYRIC—" flips the beginning of a famous Seamus Heaney quote on the potentialities of poetry for its title: "In one sense, the efficacy of poetry is nil—no lyric has ever stopped a tank."

"IT'S IMPORTANT I REMEMBER THAT PEOPLE WHO SEARCH FOR ME ON GOOGLE ALSO SEARCH FOR TERRANCE HAYES—" cites the names of several poets. These poets were selected based upon a summary of frequent Google queries that were related to searching my own name on the search engine.

"IT'S IMPORTANT I REMEMBER THAT DROPPING A BOMB ON AN OCCUPIED ROW HOUSE IS UNCONSCIONABLE—" revisits the bombing of MOVE, a Black liberation organization, by the Philadelphia Police Department on May 13, 1985. Six adults and five children were killed in the bombing, and the fire that raged in the aftermath destroyed over sixty homes on two blocks, leaving 250 people unhoused. Ramona Africa, the only surviving MOVE member, was convicted on charges of riot and conspiracy and served seven years in prison. After a civil lawsuit in federal court in 1996, the City of Philadelphia was deemed to have used excessive force and violated constitutional protections against unreasonable search and seizure; Ramona Africa and two relatives of bombing victims were awarded damages of $1.5 million. The City of Philadelphia faced another verdict in 2005 that awarded over $12 million to victims displaced by the fire after the bombing. In 2020, thirty-five years after the bombing, the Philadelphia City Council passed a resolution to formally apologize for "immeasurable and enduring harm" from the bombing and establish May 13 as a day of "observation, reflection and recommitment."

"IT'S IMPORTANT I REMEMBER THAT NELSON MANDELA WASN'T NONVIOLENT—" quotes Mandela's famous speech "I Am Prepared to Die," delivered from the defendant's dock during the Rivonia Trial. The trial imprisoned Nelson Mandela, among others, for nearly thirty years after he was convicted for sabotage against state property (on a life sentence). The Rivonia Trial marked an important inflection point in the fight against apartheid and is often referred to as "the trial that changed South Africa."

"IT'S IMPORTANT I REMEMBER THAT I'M NOT BUILT FOR THIS FIGHT—" makes a nod to Lorraine Hansberry, who wrote, while battling cancer, that she might travel to the South to "find out what kind of revolutionary I am." Hansberry, near the end of her life, believed an increasing radicalism was needed for the Black freedom struggle but harbored some self-doubt, per her journal, about how far she personally was willing to go, how much she would sacrifice. Hansberry, sadly, succumbed to cancer before she ever got the chance to head south.

"IT'S IMPORTANT I REMEMBER THAT FASCISM DIDN'T COME TO AMERICA, IT WAS ALREADY HERE—" makes partial use of the quote "When Fascism comes to America, it will be wrapped in a flag and carrying a cross." The quote is popularly attributed to author Sinclair Lewis, but there is no concrete evidence he said or penned this.

"IT'S IMPORTANT I REMEMBER THAT GOOD ARTISTS COPY—" concludes with an allusion to American race law's influence on the development of Nazi Germany's infamous Nuremberg Laws, which were used to persecute Jews and other undesirable minorities leading up to and during the Holocaust. The historical linkages are explored by author and attorney James Q. Whitman, a Yale professor, in the book *Hitler's American Model: The United States and the Making of Nazi Race Law*.

"IT'S IMPORTANT I REMEMBER THAT HARRY S. TRUMAN WAS PRESENTED WITH FOUR OPTIONS—" quotes President Harry S. Truman's telegram in response to the pleas of nationally influential minister Samuel McCrea Cavert for the US Armed Forces to cease the atomic bombing of Japan. Truman's message is dated August 11, 1945, two days after the bombing of Nagasaki. Japanese surrender was announced on August 15, 1945, by Emperor Hirohito (Emperor Shōwa).

The title "IT'S IMPORTANT I REMEMBER THAT THEY HATE US FOR OUR FREEDOM—" is an allusion to President George W. Bush's speech to a joint session of Congress on September 20, 2001, nine days after the September 11 terrorist attacks. In this speech, President Bush declared that "freedom and fear are at war." This essentially marked the beginning of what would come to be called the *war on terror*, which has cost hundreds of thousands of military and civilian lives and billions upon billions of dollars.

"IT'S IMPORTANT I REMEMBER THAT AMERICA IS FULL OF SHIT—" revisits the 1889 Navassa Revolt, its historical underpinnings, and its implications for American imperialist intent.

"IT'S IMPORTANT I REMEMBER THAT PALESTINIANS KNOW OUR POLICE BETTER THAN WE DO—" alludes to Assata Shakur's poem "Love" and pays homage to Black-Palestinian solidarity as notably exampled during the Ferguson uprising following the murder of Michael Brown by police officer Darren Wilson.

"IT'S IMPORTANT I REMEMBER THAT THOMAS JEFFERSON WAS A RAPIST—" recites the epitaph engraved on President Thomas Jefferson's tombstone. The text was chosen by Jefferson himself prior to his death.

"IT'S IMPORTANT I REMEMBER THAT ABRAHAM LINCOLN ALWAYS MEASURED BEFORE HE CUT—" paraphrases President Abraham Lincoln's correspondence (dated August 22, 1862) to Horace Greeley, the influential editor of the *New York Tribune*, expressing his preeminent goal in the American Civil War was to preserve the Union; the implication is that he was not waging an abolitionist crusade in fighting the war and considered emancipation of any (or all) enslaved people only as a political and military cudgel to be used against the Confederacy.

"IT'S IMPORTANT I REMEMBER THAT TONI MORRISON DUBBED BILL CLINTON THE FIRST BLACK PRESIDENT—" is inspired by a piece of writing Toni Morrison contributed to *The New Yorker* that stated, "White skin notwithstanding, this is our first black President. Blacker than any actual black person who could ever be elected in our children's lifetime." The purpose of Morrison writing this, which came on the heels of the impeachment investigation into Clinton's affair with White House intern Monica Lewinsky, was not to compliment the president in any way regarding his political sensibilities or his knowledge of and affinities for cultural productions that are Black in origin; this has been a very popular and long-lasting misinterpretation. Morrison, rather, was commenting on the way investigative powers were being used against Clinton and drawing parallels between his conduct and personal biography that bore similarity to tropes, both common and stereotypical, of Black lived experiences in the United States. Morrison deftly used Clinton's example to talk about power and the limitations placed upon Black people given what even the most famous white man in America—bearing great yet superficial similarities to Black people in America's cultural imagination—was subjected to despite his white skin.

"IT'S IMPORTANT I REMEMBER THAT JOURNALISM IS THE FIRST DRAFT OF HISTORY—" revolves around a retelling of the lynching of Thomas Moss and its role in inspiring Ida B. Wells to document the true horror of lynching across the United States. The poem truncates/paraphrases the last words of Thomas Moss as reported in local newspapers at the time: "Tell my people to go West, there is no justice for them here." There are also allusions to Ida B. Wells's writings in the poem, specifically her pamphlet *The Red Record*.

"IT'S IMPORTANT I REMEMBER THAT NINA SIMONE WROTE 'MISSISSIPPI GODDAM' IN LESS THAN ONE HOUR—" concludes with a retelling of Southern radio stations returning promotional singles of the protest song "Mississippi Goddam" back to Nina Simone's record label broken in half to show their disdain for its message. This did, in fact, occur and was not a purely poetic invention.

"IT'S IMPORTANT I REMEMBER THAT AMERICA EXISTS BY A KIND OF GRACE—" references the names of several locations where extreme acts of racial terror have occurred within the United States over the course of its history. It includes historic sites of violence against not only Blacks and African Americans but also against Native American and other nonwhite communities.

"IT'S IMPORTANT I REMEMBER THAT HISTORY DOESN'T REPEAT, IT RHYMES—" plays off an aphorism in its title that is frequently attributed to Mark Twain: "History never repeats itself, but it does often rhyme." The poem also uses an overheard quote from a juror in the trial of J. W. Milam and Roy Bryant in the murder of Emmett Till. Till's murderers were acquitted by an all-white, all-male jury after only sixty-seven minutes of deliberation. Neither of the men or Carol Bryant, whose claim that the fourteen-year-old Till made an inappropriate advance toward her led to his murder, ever served time in prison for the crime.

"IT'S IMPORTANT I REMEMBER THAT THERE'S A DIFFERENCE BETWEEN A HUMAN BEING AND A PERSON—" revisits a scene from the Francis Ford Coppola–directed film *The Godfather*. In the scene, Don Giuseppe discusses the potential sale of narcotics in New York and how the narcotics are only fit to be distributed for sale within Black neighborhoods due to his belief of their innate inferiority.

"IT'S IMPORTANT I REMEMBER THAT THEY DON'T HAVE THE TOOLS TO CRITIQUE ME—" references multiple Black women poets only by their first name. Though well known and thus largely discernible in the text, they are listed here for clarity in order of appearance: Lyrae Van Clief-Stefanon, Gwendolyn Brooks, Lucille Clifton, and June Jordan. This poem is also a tribute to Cave Canem, the fellowship founded by Toi Derricotte and Cornelius Eady to foster the artistic growth of Black poets.

"IT'S IMPORTANT I REMEMBER THAT THE RIGHT TO KEEP AND BEAR ARMS IS THE SECOND AMENDMENT—" lifts a line of text directly from the Second Amendment of the United States Constitution.

"IT'S IMPORTANT I REMEMBER THAT IT COSTS EXTRA TO ADD CHEESE ON A WHOPPER—" riffs on lyrics from the Big L song "No Endz, No Skinz" from his debut album, *Lifestylez ov da Poor & Dangerous*.

"IT'S IMPORTANT I REMEMBER THAT GEORGE ZIMMERMAN ISN'T WHITE—" was inspired by George Zimmerman auctioning off the gun he used to kill Trayvon Martin. The weapon was ultimately sold for $250,000. Zimmerman, while promoting the auction, described the gun as "a piece of American history."

"IT'S IMPORTANT I REMEMBER THAT PEOPLE VOTED FOR DONALD TRUMP BECAUSE OF ECONOMIC ANXIETY—" includes a citation of exit polling data conducted by Edison Research for the National Election Pool, a consortium of ABC News, the Associated Press, CBS News, CNN, Fox News, and NBC News.

"IT'S IMPORTANT I REMEMBER THAT SOJOURNER TRUTH HADN'T SUFFERED ENOUGH—" makes references to two transcriptions of a speech Sojourner Truth delivered at the Women's Rights Convention at Old Stone Church in Akron, Ohio, in 1851. "Ain't I a Woman?" is the more famous transcription and was published by Frances Dana Barker Gage in 1863, twelve years after the speech was made. In this version, Gage made several changes to the voice and personal background of Sojourner Truth to make it more palatable to white, Northern audiences. Another, more accurate, transcription of the speech titled "I Am a Woman's Rights" reported by newspapers of the time is also referenced in the poem. Finally, the poem closes by spinning a phrase that Truth used on the back of photographs of herself she sold to fund her advocacy: "I sell the shadow to support the substance."

"IT'S IMPORTANT I REMEMBER THAT FANNIE LOU HAMER KEPT THE PHONE OFF THE HOOK—" was, in part, inspired by the poem "Fannie Lou Hamer" by the late Kamilah Aisha Moon. Both poems refer to Fannie Lou Hamer's speech before the credentials committee of the 1964 Democratic National Convention but otherwise cover different (yet thematically related) terrain.

"IT'S IMPORTANT I REMEMBER THAT ELLA BAKER WAS MARRIED TO THE MOVEMENT—" directly quotes Ella Baker ("Strong people don't need strong leaders").

"IT'S IMPORTANT I REMEMBER THAT HALLE BERRY IS THE ONLY BLACK WOMAN TO WIN AN ACADEMY AWARD FOR BEST ACTRESS—" lifts a quote from the 2003 film *Monster's Ball*, starring Halle Berry. The borrowed line ("I'm a bad man. You're the best of me.") is delivered by Sean "Diddy" Combs playing the character of Lawrence, awaiting execution on death row, speaking to his son Tyrell, whom he fathered with Halle Berry's character, Leticia.

"IT'S IMPORTANT I REMEMBER THAT I BELIEVED I COULD FLY—" references the names Robert and Michael. These are the singer R. Kelly and Chicago Bulls legend Michael Jordan, respectively.

"IT'S IMPORTANT I REMEMBER THAT LOVE PRESUMES PROTECTION—" references a Maya at the beginning. This refers to poet Maya Marshall and her appearance on Poetry Foundation's *VS* podcast ("Maya Marshall vs. Priorities"), hosted by Ajanaé Dawkins and Brittany Rogers. The episode was released on January 31, 2023.

"IT'S IMPORTANT I REMEMBER THAT JAY-Z ARRIVED ON THE DAY FRED HAMPTON DIED—" both directly and indirectly references Jay-Z lyrics from the songs "Murder to Excellence" (from the collaborative album with Kanye West, *Watch the Throne*), "Dead Presidents II" (from Jay-Z's solo album *Reasonable Doubt*), "Family Feud" (from Jay-Z's solo album *4:44*), and "Moment of Clarity" (from Jay-Z's solo album *The Black Album*). The poem also directly quotes Fred Hampton, chairman of the Illinois Chapter of the Black Panther Party, who was assassinated by the Chicago Police Department in 1969.

"IT'S IMPORTANT I REMEMBER THAT KANYE WEST DOESN'T CARE ABOUT BLACK PEOPLE—" playfully uses Kanye West's comments about slavery "sound[ing] like a choice." West intended these words as meaning Black people play into their own subjugation; it is an ahistorical statement that diminishes a tremendously long history of Black resistance.

"IT'S IMPORTANT I REMEMBER THAT I'M AVOIDING THE FOOTAGE—" names six people by first name only. These six people are Tyre Nichols and the five Memphis police officers who killed him: Tadarrius Bean, Justin Smith, Demetrius Haley, Emmitt Martin III, and Desmond Mills Jr. All five officers were Black, as was Nichols.

"IT'S IMPORTANT I REMEMBER THAT PARTING IS SUCH SWEET SORROW—" is a poetic consideration of the eventual lead organizer behind the March on Washington for Jobs and Freedom, Bayard Rustin, and his ouster from the inner circle of advisors to Dr. Martin Luther King Jr. ahead of the 1960 Democratic National Convention due to the threat of blackmail from Rep. Adam Clayton Powell Jr. over Rustin's homosexuality. Powell was attempting to fend off a public demonstration by MLK and the Southern Christian Leadership Conference at the Democratic National Convention, which would have been politically costly to Powell.

"IT'S IMPORTANT I REMEMBER THAT ONE BLACK JUSTICE REPLACED ANOTHER—" has a brief allusion to Anita Hill, who publicly testified about sexual harassment she suffered at the hands of Clarence Thomas during his confirmation hearings for the Supreme Court.

"IT'S IMPORTANT I REMEMBER THAT THERE'S ALWAYS HOPE—" is a cento of one hundred lines that draws text from one hundred poets (featuring one of my own previous lines plus one line each from ninety-nine other poets). The poets who were referenced to create the cento are listed here in order of appearance: Ocean Vuong; Eve L. Ewing; Sonia Sanchez; Sumita Chakraborty; Patricia Smith; Ross Gay; Natasha Trethewey; Galway Kinnel; Stanley Kunitz; Patricia Fargnoli; Angel Nafis; May Swenson; June Jordan; Jorie Graham; Linda Gregg; Jane Hirshfield; Elizabeth Alexander; Cortney Lamar Charleston (me); Aracelis Girmay; Allison Hedge Coke; Mary Oliver; Natalie Diaz; Sharon Olds; Eduardo C. Corral; Kim Addonizio; Gwendolyn Brooks; Emily Dickinson; Eloisa Amezcua; Matthew Olzmann; William E. Stafford; Shane McCrae; Wendell Berry; Evie Shockley; Rachel McKibbens; Lucille Clifton; Parneshia Jones; Adrienne Rich; e. e. cummings; Li-Young Lee; Jack Gilbert; Juan Felipe Herrera; Francisco X. Alarcón; C. P. Cavafy; Olena Kalytiak Davis; Solmaz Sharif; Rick Barot; Aria Aber; Layli Long Soldier; Allen Ginsberg; W. S. Merwin; Gabrielle Calvocoressi; Amiri Baraka; Lyrae Van Clief-Stefanon; Robert Frost; Toi Derricotte; Naomi Shihab Nye; Tracy K. Smith; Miller Williams; Jericho Brown; Joy Harjo; Claudia Rankine; Wisława Szymborska; Hayden Carruth;

Kathryn Starbuck; Frank O'Hara; Maya Angelou; Thylias Moss; Phillis Wheatley; Morgan Parker; Khadijah Queen; Suji Kwock Kim; Diane di Prima; William Wordsworth; Kimiko Hahn; Wendy Xu; Jameson Fitzpatrick; Hala Alyan; D. A. Powell; Jamaal May; Yusef Komunyakaa; Richard Blanco; Danez Smith; Ada Limón; Rita Dove; Cathy Linh Che; Marilyn Chin; Aditi Machado; Safia Elhillo; Vievee Francis; Nikki Giovanni; Tyree Daye; Terrance Hayes; Joy Ladin; Donika Kelly; francine j. harris; Marge Piercy; Ginger Ko; Gerard Manley Hopkins; Frank Bidart; and Nicole Sealey.

"IT'S IMPORTANT I REMEMBER THAT THE MAJORITY OF AMERICANS AGREE THE COUNTRY IS ON THE WRONG TRACK—" was created by referencing the findings of public opinion polling conducted after Donald Trump's breakthrough in national politics as the leading Republican candidate for president and throughout his first presidency from 2017 through 2021.

"IT'S IMPORTANT I REMEMBER THAT DONALD TRUMP'S SUPPORTERS ATTACKING THE CAPITOL WAS UNPRECEDENTED, NOT UNPREDICTABLE—" features a section composed of unattributed quotations from Donald Trump as made in public speeches or reported in mainstream American media during his time in presidential politics.

ACKNOWLEDGMENTS

Where am I to start my enumerations of gratitude? I guess it's best to begin with the people who were with me at my beginning: my family. My love and appreciation go to my parents, Pamela and Vincent, and to my grandparents, George and Joan and Gomez and Margie, whose spirits and life lessons orient both the heart and the mind behind this book. I send my love to my siblings, whose belief in me continues to be a sustaining force: Cameron, Camille, Calah. And shout out to my aunties and uncles, and to all my cousins for giving me a tribe to call my own.

Knowingly, none of what I write—with all its joys and moonlit agonies—is possible without my wife, Ruani, devotedly uplifting me, steadying me, and ensuring that I recognize and honor the contributions I make to the lives of those around me, especially in moments of profound self-doubt. And to our gleeful little boy, Liam, I surrender my best self and thank you for allowing me to see the world anew, through your eyes, which I understand is essential to its reimagining and remaking as a more just and compassionate place.

To the Excelano Project: I will forever be in your debt for bringing me into poetry. Thank you, dear poets, for your example and the legacy we all are contributing to. March forth!

To Cave Canem: Our fellowship, the binding of our many selves to the craft and to one another, is precious to me. You've given me a confidence of voice and vision I'd no longer recognize myself without. You've brought me more fully into a life of poetry; for this, I thank you.

Any of the poets in my communities can tell you that composing a collection is a largely solitary endeavor, but that's likewise what makes moments of collaborative intervention that inspire or instruct so special. I have enduring gratitude to the wonderful poets and thinkers who encouraged me in the infancy of this project and provided insight that informed how the text you're reading now was brought to completion: Claire Schwartz and Isaac Ginsberg Miller, thank you.

Thank you, also, to the poets who point the way forward for me—artistically and/or politically—in ways that shaped this specific collection, some having generously given time to this work in whole or part prior to its publication: Ariana Benson,

Aricka Foreman, Aurielle Marie, Camonghne Felix, Carolina Ebeid, Claudia Rankine, Clint Smith, D. A. Powell, Danez Smith, Emily Jungmin Yoon, Eve L. Ewing, Evie Shockley, Fatimah Asghar, Franny Choi, George Abraham, Honorée Fanonne Jeffers, Jericho Brown, José Olivarez, Joy Priest, Julian Randall, Kaveh Akbar, Kyle Dargan, Lyrae Van Clief-Stefanon, Mahogany L. Browne, Marwa Helal, Maya Marshall, Morgan Parker, Nabila Lovelace, Nate Marshall, Nicole Sealey, Patricia Smith, Roy G. Guzmán, Safia Elhillo, Sumita Chakraborty, Tara Betts, Terrance Hayes, Tyehimba Jess, Vievee Francis, Willie Perdomo. This is an illustrative list and yet still so far from exhaustive, as there are many friends and inspirations that I owe gratitude to, which I will try to express in other ways.

Speaking of exhaustion, I appreciate that the expansiveness of this poetry collection required a rare patience and an inspiring amount of belief in its merit for Northwestern University Press to publish. From the bottom of my heart, I thank Marisa Siegel for her editorial stewardship, Parneshia Jones for her faith in this project, and the incredible staff supporting its release from all angles: Christopher Bigelow, Charlotte Keathley, Courtney Smotherman, Mary Klein, Maddy Schultz, and Kristen Twardowski. This has been a triumph of genuine partnership.

Lastly, many individual poems in this collection have been graciously provided audiences by numerous periodicals prior to the publication of this book. I extend my appreciation to the publications named below who gave first homes to the poems listed, sometimes with differences:

Academy of American Poets: Poem-a-Day
"It's Important I Remember That the Moral Arc of the Universe Bends—"

Action, Spectacle
"It's Important I Remember That Ella Baker Was Married to the Movement—" • "It's Important I Remember That Jesus Wept—" • "It's Important I Remember That the Root of the Problem Is the Root—"

The Adroit Journal
"It's Important I Remember That We're Not Bearing Witness, We're Watching—"

AGNI
"It's Important I Remember That History Is All a Big Misunderstanding—" • "It's Important I Remember That Thomas Jefferson Was a Rapist—"

The American Poetry Review
"It's Important I Remember That Fannie Lou Hamer Kept the Phone Off the Hook—"

The Atlantic
"It's Important I Remember That Nina Simone Wrote 'Mississippi Goddam' in Less Than One Hour—"

Beloit Poetry Journal
"It's Important I Remember That Politics Is a Contact Sport—"

Bennington Review
"It's Important I Remember That the Obamas' First Date Was Seeing *Do the Right Thing*—"

Borderlands: Texas Poetry Review
"It's Important I Remember That Even Donald Trump Didn't Believe He'd Win the Election—"

The Cincinnati Review
"It's Important I Remember That *Darkness* and *Blackness* Aren't Perfect Synonyms—" • "It's Important I Remember That Enslaved People Married Here—"

The Common
"It's Important I Remember That Fascism Didn't Come to America, It Was Already Here—" • "It's Important I Remember That Journalism Is the First Draft of History—"

The Florida Review
"It's Important I Remember That Survival Is a Matter of Luck—"

Glass: A Journal of Poetry
"It's Important I Remember That a Tank Has Never Stopped the Lyric—"

Grist: A Journal of the Literary Arts
"It's Important I Remember That Halle Berry Is the Only Black Woman to Win an Academy Award for Best Actress—"

Guernica: A Magazine of Global Art and Politics
"It's Important I Remember That Things Are Getting Back to Normal Around Here—"

Gulf Coast: A Journal of Literature and Fine Arts
"It's Important I Remember That the Majority of Americans Agree the Country Is on the Wrong Track—"

Hoxie Gorge Review
"It's Important I Remember That the Final Scene of *Django Unchained* Is the Destruction of Candyland—" • "It's Important I Remember That the Right to Keep and Bear Arms Is the Second Amendment—"

In These Times
"It's Important I Remember That I'm Avoiding the Footage—" • "It's Important I Remember That My Employer Cares About My Safety and Well-Being—"

jubilat
"It's Important I Remember That It Costs Extra to Add Cheese on a Whopper—"

The Massachusetts Review
"It's Important I Remember That Dropping a Bomb on an Occupied Row House Is Unconscionable—" • "It's Important I Remember That Orange Is the New Black—"

Mississippi Review
"It's Important I Remember That I'm Not Built for This Fight—" • "It's Important I Remember That Lyndon B. Johnson Said, 'We Have Lost the South for a Generation'—" • "It's Important I Remember That One Black Justice Replaced Another—" • "It's Important I Remember That South Carolina Seceded First—"

The Nation
"It's Important I Remember That There's a Difference Between a Human Being and a Person—"

New England Review
"It's Important I Remember That Abraham Lincoln Always Measured Before He Cut—" • "It's Important I Remember That Frederick Douglass Learned How to Read—"

New Letters
"It's Important I Remember That Sojourner Truth Hadn't Suffered Enough—" • "It's Important I Remember That the Enemy of My Enemy Is Someone I Don't Know Very Well—"

POETRY
"It's Important I Remember That They Don't Have the Tools to Critique Me—"

Poetry London
"It's Important I Remember That the United States Hasn't Issued a Declaration of War Since World War II—"

Poet Lore
"It's Important I Remember That Parting Is Such Sweet Sorrow—"

Poetry Northwest
"It's Important I Remember—" • "It's Important I Remember That America Exists by a Kind of Grace—" • "It's Important I Remember That Whiteness Is Only an Orientation—"

The Poetry Review
"It's Important I Remember That There Is No Universally Recognized Definition—"

Puerto del Sol
"It's Important I Remember That History Doesn't Repeat, It Rhymes—" • "It's Important I Remember That Twista Can Make You a Celebrity Overnight—"

Salamander
"It's Important I Remember That I Can Never Wash My Hands Enough—" • "It's Important I Remember That There Are Several Ways to Kill Houseplants—"

Shō Poetry Journal
"It's Important I Remember That Being Alone and Being Lonely Aren't the Same Thing—" • "It's Important I Remember That Even Beyoncé Got Cheated On—"

SLICE
"It's Important I Remember That I Believed I Could Fly—"

Southeast Review
"It's Important I Remember That a Current Event Is a Current—" • "It's Important I Remember That in Order for White People to Study My Life, They Must First Study My Body—"

Southern Indiana Review
"It's Important I Remember That the Feeling of an Eye on Me Burns—" • "It's Important I Remember That the Only Thing We Have to Fear Is Fear Itself—"

TriQuarterly
"It's Important I Remember That All I Have to Do Is Stay Black and Die—" • "It's Important I Remember That Jay-Z Arrived on the Day Fred Hampton Died—" • "It's Important I Remember That Toni Morrison Dubbed Bill Clinton the First Black President—"

Waxwing
"It's Important I Remember That George Zimmerman Isn't White—" • "It's Important I Remember That Kanye West Doesn't Care About Black People—" • "It's Important I Remember That People Who Search for Me on Google Also Search for Terrance Hayes—"

Furthermore, the poetic sequence "It's Important I Remember That There Was No Poet at Donald Trump's Inauguration—" features two excerpts from famed Spanish poet Federico García Lorca's *Theory and Play of the Duende*, as translated by A. S. Kline. I extend my profound gratitude to Casanovas and Lynch, who manage permissions for Lorca's estate in Spain, and Adam Kline for their permission to use these words in this artistic project. The aforementioned sequence was also an evolution from an early piece of writing titled "Aria from the Arena," which was written for the Poetry Society of America.

Finally, the poetic sequence "It's Important I Remember That People Voted for Donald Trump Because of Economic Anxiety—" was also an evolution of an earlier composition simply titled "Economic Anxiety," which was originally published by *Lunch Ticket*, based at Antioch University Los Angeles.